CHICLE

CHICLE

THE CHEWING GUM OF THE AMERICAS,
FROM THE ANCIENT MAYA TO WILLIAM WRIGLEY

JENNIFER P. MATHEWS
with
GILLIAN P. SCHULTZ

The University of Arizona Press   Tucson

The University of Arizona Press
© 2009 The Arizona Board of Regents
All rights reserved

www.uapress.arizona.edu

Library of Congress Cataloging-in-Publication Data
Mathews, Jennifer P., 1969-
    Chicle : the chewing gum of the Americas, from the ancient Maya to William Wrigley /
    Jennifer P. Mathews ; with Gillian P. Schultz.
        p. cm.
    Includes bibliographical references and index.
ISBN 978-0-8165-2624-6 (hardcover : alk. paper) —
ISBN 978-0-8165-2821-9 (pbk. : alk. paper)
    1. Sapodilla. 2. Chewing gum—Central America—History. 3. Chewing gum—Mexico—
    History. 4. Chewing gum—United States—History. 5. Chewing gum—Social aspects—
    America—History. 6. Chewing gum industry—America—History. 7. Chicle—Industrial
    applications—History. I. Schultz, Gillian P. II. Title. SB291.S3M38 2009
664'.6—dc22

                                                              2008051922

Manufactured in the United States of America on acid-free, archival-quality paper
containing a minimum of 30% post-consumer waste and processed chlorine free.

14   13   12   11   10   09   6   5   4   3   2   1

CONTENTS

ILLUSTRATIONS

ACKNOWLEDGMENTS

This book may seem a bit off topic for a Maya archaeologist to be writing, but it stemmed from a long-term project that started when my then advisor Scott Fedick and I stumbled upon a section of chicle railroad near Puerto Morelos, Quintana Roo, in 1995. Over the next several years, I returned to map the 40 km railroad that led from the coast to the chicle camp of Santa María. From there I began my decade-long journey of studying chicle.

First I need to thank all of the members of the Yalahau Regional Human Ecology Project who have become my family away from home. In particular I want to give special thanks to those who helped me with all of the fieldwork over the years and slogged through the jungle, slept in hammocks and on bad beds and cots, got lost on back roads and jungle trails, put up with snakes, chiggers, and chechem, dealt with our seemingly unending supply of bad field vehicles (through all the flat tires, gas fumes, doors that fell off, and engine problems), and drank warm Leon Negras without complaint. Project members included Evan Bitto, Jorge Ceja-Acosta, Augustine Chapin, Jessica Dahlberg, Claudia DesLaurier, Matt DesLaurier, Leigh-Ann Ellison, Chris Ganno, Melissa García, Aaron Gardner, Kim Goldsmith-Jilote, Anna Hoover, Tamzin Howerton, Reiko Ishihara, Cody Johns, Jordan Kindiger, Connie López-Marx, Karl Lorenzen, Chase Milam, Ben Miller, Katherine Moore, Kasey Moreland, Matthew Morriarty, Helen Neylan, Lori Navarette, Jana Perser, Holly Prosser, Dawn Reid, Jean Schwab, Carlos Santos-Coy, Dennis Taylor, Darcy Wiewall, and Susan Winzler (with apologies to anyone I have forgotten). In particular, I want to send out a big "Xpu-Ha" to several of my closest fieldwork friends with whom I have had some of the best times of my life: Bente Andersen, Julie Bell, Fabio Esteban-Amador, Olivia Navarro-Farr, Jeffrey Glover, Kurt Heidelberg, Charles Houck, Kevin Hovey, Scott Hutson, Josh Kwoka, Carole Leezer, Lilia Lizama-Rogers, Maggie Moore, Shanti Morell-Hart, Bethany Morrison, Dominique Rissolo, Greg Smith, and Kathy Sorensen.

All fieldwork in Mexico was conducted under permit by the Instituto Nacional de Antropología e Historia. I would like to thank the INAH Consejo for granting us permission to work in Quintana Roo since 1993. I would also like to single out several INAH archaeologists who have helped me out over the years: Sylviane Boucher, María José Con-Uribe, Rach Cobos, Rubén Maldonaldo, Tómas Gallareta-Negron, and Adriana Velázquez.

I have had the privilege of interviewing many former chicleros who were in their seventies and eighties, as well as their family members. They let me into their houses, shared their vivid stories and their photographs. I am so glad that I've had the chance to hear their tales and to share them in this book. I'd like to recognize Don Demetio Acosta Pérez, Honorio Aguilar, Don Florentino Chacom, Juana Maria Chacom, Don Mario Hernández Lorenzo, José Montoya, Don Juan Montoya, Don Tómas Nuñez, Jorge Ramos, and Don Alberto Sánchez for their willingness to pass on this history. I would especially like to thank my friend Rosa Poot Pool for her companionship, contagious laugh, and wonderful meals over the years. I also need to single out Lilia Lizama-Rogers and Bill Rogers for all of their help in introducing me to many of the people of the area and for their friendship through the years.

This fieldwork could not have been conducted without the help and financial support of several agencies and people. Thank you to the Foundation for the Advancement of Mesoamerican Studies, Inc. (Award #98027), the National Science Foundation Grant (Award #SBR–9600956), Trinity University and the Department of Sociology and Anthropology, Mike and Theresa Baker of the Baker Family Foundation, and Charles Bush (aka "Bush") and Gail Darden for sponsoring several aspects of fieldwork related to this long-term project. I would also like to say a special thank you to Dr. Peter D. and Alexandra M. Harrison for their enthusiasm and generous financial support for helping to publish this manuscript. Peter, it has always been an honor working with you.

I cannot thank the talented Macduff Everton enough for the use of his beautiful photographs for this book. I have greatly admired your work for years, and it has been a thrill to be able to include your images in this volume. You and your staff have been such a pleasure to work with, and your incredible photographs have added so much to this work.

Thank you to Allyson Carter and Christine Szuter of the University of Arizona Press. You have now seen me through three book projects and have been so encouraging for each of them. I appreciate your continued support and look forward to the next book project. The proposal will be in the mail soon.

Several colleagues assisted me with many aspects of the research of this book. I want to note my appreciation for help and expertise to: my former advisor Karl Taube for always sharing his library and encyclopedic knowledge on all things pre-Columbian; Francis Berdan for references to Aztec codices and contact-period manuscripts; David Stuart for his thoughts on the ancient use of chicle; James Brady for helpful suggestions and publications on rubber; Rosana Caño-Blanco for her help with chicle-related Spanish phrases; Norman Schwartz for his incredibly important work on chicleros and the chicle industry—I truly look forward to our continuing collaboration on future chicle-related projects; Nicolle Hirschfeld for her recommendations in dealing with classical texts; Mia Taylor, finder of lost quotes and the most amazing online researcher that I've ever met—you saved me hours of hair-pulling and made life infinitely easier on multiple occasions; and Paul Sullivan for providing a number of useful references and historical maps. A big thank you to Justine Shaw for reading an earlier draft of the manuscript and providing always-useful suggestions. You continue to be one of the easiest people with whom I've ever worked. Thank you also to the anonymous reviewers who provided thoughtful feedback and truly shaped the direction of this book.

Sincere thanks to several people who assisted with the research process: Clint Chamberlain, Janice Sabec, and the library staff at Trinity's Coates Library for help with locating sources; Pat Ullmann in the Center for Learning and Technology at Trinity for assistance with creating several of the figures; Maria McWilliams and the Inter-Library Loan staff for ordering so many articles and books and getting them to me so quickly; Deborah Schimberg of Verve, Inc. for providing information about the contemporary chicle industry; and Elizabeth Harvey of the Brooklyn Collection at the Brooklyn Public Library for allowing me access to the archives and finding so many little gems in the archives of the *Daily Eagle*.

I have always been blessed with wonderful friends and family and I have many to thank here. To my Trinity friends Bert Chandler, Dan Spiegel, and of course Carolyn Becker. I so appreciate your friendship, support, and fellow love of appetizers and drinks on the patio. You—and the rest of the Beer Tuesday crowd—put the fun in work. I cannot forget my oldest friends, Jeanette Anderson, Micah Fox, Mark Griffiths, Michelle Harlan, Danielle Kamian, Lizi Thompson, and Renee Winchell. Although we have all taken divergent paths, I am so lucky that we grew up together, survived the 1980s together, and look forward to growing old together. Thank you for always being in my life and for reminding me that I'm still a kid on the inside.

When it came time to writing the botany chapter of this book I realized that I was in over my head. Thankfully, my graduate school friend Gill Schultz had the expertise I needed, and we had been looking for an excuse to work together for years. She proved to be a wonderful collaborator and showed endless patience with my never-ending questions and suggested revisions. Thank you so much for being willing to work with me on this—and for adding a critical chapter to this volume. I am grateful for all of your help—but I most want to thank you for our years of friendship, *Melrose Place*, ice-skating, and Latin dance contests.

Since I first stepped foot on the UC Riverside campus back in 1992, Scott Fedick has been one of the most important people in my life. Thank you for always pushing me beyond my comfort zone and holding me to such high standards in the classroom and in the field. Your friendship, mentorship, advice, support, and the opportunities that you provided are some of the biggest reasons that I made it through grad school, got a job and tenure. I'm sure there is a place in the afterlife waiting for you with a 1969 Landcruiser that never breaks down, daily estate sales, and a Mexican hot dog cart that never runs out of Scott Dogs.

To my dear friend Dominique (Box Ni) Rissolo, I want to express my gratitude for over twenty years of friendship. I can't tell you how much I appreciate the fact that you always drank the *chac pol* at the fiestas in Naranjal, got us through the Mexican cow mishap and was there to eat gopher guts with me, dropped me into caves and cenotes, have shared Zoë, Enzo, Dario, and Emilio with me, and that you always seemed to be there to get me through the hard parts of everything. If I had a brother, I would want it to be you. A huge *abrazo* to my best friend in the world, Ramona Pérez. You opened up your family and home to me, have been my closest confidante and advice counselor, office mate, dissertation editor, copilot, and my superhero. I admire your intellect, drive, passion, and love of life. I will always treasure our many *aventuras* and look forward to our continuous quest to find the perfect Cuba Libre.

To my big crazy family—the Guthries, Lowrys, Mathews, Mullers, Phillipses, Peytons, and Smeds—I want you to know that I love you all very much and thank you for always putting an emphasis on family. I especially want to thank my grandmas Marjorie Mathews and Elsie Lowry. Your spirits have guided me long after you left—and I am forever grateful for the time that we had together. To Gary Withrow—thank you for being so good to my mom, Opie, and me for the last twenty-plus years. We are lucky to have you in our lives. To my wicked stepmother Alison Turner—I could not have asked for a more supportive or loving addition to my family. Thank you for always being one of my biggest cheerleaders and such an important figure in my life. You make wicked look good. To my mama, Cyndie Lowry—you have given up so much so that I could pursue my education and my career and I could have never done it without you. You will never know how much that has meant to me, and I am the luckiest daughter to have you in my life. I love you to the moon and back. (You too Sheesha.) To Lou Mathews, who is the coolest dad on the earth. I know that I've always been a daddy's girl, but there aren't too many fathers and daughters who could spend three weeks together driving through Mexico in a beat-up Jeep and come out closer for it. You gave me my travel bug, my love of food, and a passion for writing, and I will always love you for it. I can also not thank you enough for reading through this manuscript (over and over again) and making it a much better book. This is as much your book as it is mine. You are a remarkable person, an extraordinarily patient editor, and a brilliant writing teacher.

To Gabi Huesca, it has been such a joy to see you grow up from a little girl to an intelligent, beautiful young woman. I'm so glad that you have been such an important part of my life. My love and gratitude goes out to Roberto Huesca for being my friend and partner of many years. I have learned so much from you, and no matter how much time has passed, no one can make me laugh or enjoy life the way you do. Lastly, I want to thank Mrs. B. for being my constant companion while I wrote this book. My desk could be absolutely cluttered with papers and books, but it would feel empty without her curled up next to my laptop.

CHICLE

INTRODUCTION

Although chewing gum has been a part of North American popular culture for over a century, few consumers know the history of this product: neither its use by pre-Columbian cultures such as the Aztec and Maya, nor its extraction for mass consumption by global markets. This volume is an 11,000-year overview of chewing gum. In particular, it focuses on chicle (the resin used in chewing gum), from its earliest uses among pre-contact peoples to the boom and bust extraction industry of the nineteenth and twentieth centuries and its small-scale use today. This research has been done through the use of historical documents and photographs, anthropological, archaeological, botanical, and cultural ecological literature, ethnographic interviews with contemporary *chicleros* (chicle extractors), and on-the-ground archaeology. I would like to emphasize that although this volume is a discussion of chicle in the "Americas," it is almost entirely focused on the United States, Mexico, Guatemala, and Belize, as this is where the overwhelming majority of the chicle extraction and industry has been located. Finally, extensive notes are provided for those who are looking for the citation information, or for additional resources related to the discussions in the main text.

Chapter 1 examines the broader use of the sapodilla tree (from which we extract chicle) through time in the Americas. Some tropical tree barks secrete latex, like chicle, within specialized ducts, and extractors harvest them by cutting into the flesh of the tree and allowing it to run down the trunk. The ancient Aztecs of Mexico chewed this natural gum, but held strict social norms about its use. While they recognized that it freshened breath, it was also a social marker of whores and "effeminates," and "respectable" adults were forbidden to chew it in public. Although the ancient Maya also chewed it as gum, they used the sapodilla in its entirety. They exploited the wood for everything from firewood and as building materials for the houses of commoners, to the carved lintels on temples. The sweet sapodilla fruits were a favored food that the Spanish prized highly after contact. Some researchers believe that Maya elites controlled the access to the trees by growing them in their city centers. Chicle latex also shares qualities with other important plant exudates such as copal resin (used primarily as incense) and rubber latex. These physical similarities, which gave each of these natural products an infinite number of utilitarian uses, likely extended to their ritual purposes as well.

Chapter 2, written in conjunction with botanist Gillian P. Schultz, presents the sapodilla tree through the lens of botany, with much of the information coming from the botanical studies that the chicle industry commissioned in the 1930s. The chapter explains the complicated nomenclature and subsequent taxonomic confusion of the species, starting with Carolus Linnaeus's first published description in 1753. The sapodilla tree, which is native only to Mesoamerica and the Caribbean, is a slow-growing but highly adaptive species. It can withstand a variety of environmental obstacles such as drought and poor drainage, and is primarily limited by colder temperatures. This adaptability has allowed for its introduction throughout the tropics of the Old World, where farmers have propagated it for its fruit since the Spanish introduced it at contact. Native peoples also use the tree products for medicinal purposes, and the fruit contains tannins (an antioxidant) and the entire plant produces saponins, which act as an antimicrobial. In the wild, sapodilla reproduction occurs primarily through bat pollination, and its distribution is dependent on animals eating the fruits and dispersing the seeds through their scat. For the sapodilla seedlings to grow, they must battle with other forest species for sunlight and nutrients. Reaching up to one hundred feet in height, these trees are highly resistant to disturbances such as hurricanes. Visitors to the forests of southern Mexico, Guatemala, and Belize can recognize the trees by the zigzagging scars left in the gray bark by chicleros in their attempt to extract the white latex.

Chapter 3 focuses on the development of chicle as an industry in the Americas, concentrating in particular on the relationship between the industry in the United States and Mexico. It tells the story of the American invention of chewing gum and the growth of an industry dominated for much of the twentieth century by such companies as Adams, Wrigley, Fleer, and the American Chicle Company. Many of the major players in the industry lived colorful lives, such as Thomas Adams

Sr., the inventor of chicle-based chewing gum who first came across natural chicle resin through none other than the exiled president of Mexico, Antonio López de Santa Anna. William Wrigley Jr. left home at the age of thirteen to become a traveling soap salesman and ended up a millionaire chewing gum magnate.

Mexican and Central American officials encouraged these industrialists to extract chicle during the first half of the twentieth century through land grants and cheap labor, resulting in chicle becoming one of the largest and most important exports. The popularity of gum continued to spread with the incorporation of it into the rations of soldiers during World War I and II, hurtling annual sales to over a billion dollars. With these demands, overtapping of sapodillas became a consistent problem, and corporations began seeking out synthetic substitutes. The natural gum industry boom became a bust during the 1950s and 1960s and was nearly abandoned in the 1970s and 1980s. Today, chicle production has become a boutique industry that caters to consumers interested in natural products.

Chapter 4 focuses on the culture of chicleros and examines the stereotypes of the lone chiclero in the "wild west" of Mexico, Guatemala, and Belize, the day-to-day working conditions, and the process of chicle collecting. As the lifestyle allowed for unsupervised work in the jungles, it did attract individuals running from the law, or those shunned by their indigenous villages, although this was not the case for the majority of workers. Wages were relatively low, the workdays were long, conditions were dangerous, and chicleros often lived in debt to the company stores that provided their equipment and food at inflated prices. Outsiders often feared the chicleros when they came into town because they knew them for their excessive drinking, promiscuity, gambling, and violence. Foreign corporations afforded them little sympathy for their poor working conditions and saw them as primitive and backward. This combination of factors resulted in chiclero uprisings, further damaging their reputations. However, chicleros have also had a significant role in archaeology, as they have been responsible for the discovery of some of the most important sites in the Maya area. For over a century, archaeologists have used them as guides and workers, and if it were not for their explorations in the forest, many important sites might still be unknown. This relationship has also led to the unwitting outcome of chicleros looting many of the same sites that they discovered.

The history of the use of chicle, its subsequent botanical studies intertwined with the development of the chewing gum industry, and the life of chicleros in the Yucatán Peninsula have garnered relatively little attention in the academic literature. This volume is an attempt to provide an in-depth look at this vivid and significant history, and perhaps to shed light on the role the industry played in the working conditions of chicleros and impacts it has had on local indigenous communities.

THE BIRTH OF THE CHEWING GUM TREE

> But the bad women, those called harlots, [show] no fine feelings; quite
> publicly they go about chewing chicle along the roads, in the market place,
> clacking like castanets.
> —Fray Bernardino de Sahagún, writing about Aztec society in the 1590s.[1]

> Dear friends, we surely all agree
> There's almost nothing worse to see
> Than some repulsive little bum
> Who's always chewing chewing gum.
> —An excerpt from a song by the Oompa Loompas in the book *Charlie
>   and the Chocolate Factory*[2]

If they think of gum at all, most people picture chewing gum in its current colorful, sweet stick or Chiclets form, a totally synthetic product that clings to the bottom of one's shoe but not in one's mind. In truth, gum precedes shoes and philosophy, with a long history that cuts across centuries and cultures, starting with bark tar that was chewed nine thousand years ago in Neolithic Europe.[3] It also derives from a widespread tradition of using natural plant exudates (a waste product that is excreted from cells) for everything from incense to embalming, and as solvents, adhesives, lacquers, and sealants.[4] This chapter will look specifically at the pre-Columbian use of natural products of the sapodilla tree, including the chicle latex, wood, and fruit and discuss the possible ritual significance of using chicle for ancient Mesoamericans.

Chicle across the Centuries

The sapodilla, or chicozapote, tree (*Manilkara zapota*) from which chicle is collected has a New World origin in southern Mexico and Central America.[5] The trees are found in the Mexican states of Chiapas, Tabasco, Veracruz, Oaxaca, Michoacán, and Colima, although they are best suited to the karst limestone region of northern Belize, the Petén region of Guatemala, and the Mexican states of Campeche, Yucatán, and Quintana Roo in the Yucatán Peninsula (see fig. 2.1).[6] The greatest concentration of indigenous sapodillas are found in Quintana Roo, and are probably the remnants of active propagation by the ancient Maya or were simply spared by ancient farmers when they cleared the forests for their fields.[7]

When the bark of the sapodilla is cut or attacked by insects, the tree produces a milky fluid that forms a protective layer over the damaged area. It is this substance, known as chicle latex, that has been used for hundreds of years in the Americas as chewing gum. Natural latexes, such as chicle and rubber, are usually a white, thick emulsion, although at times they can be clear, yellow, red, or orange and runny. Latex is produced in specialized vessels or cells of plants known as laticifers, and are made up of carbohydrates, alkaloids, and proteins. In general, they play a protective role in wounded plants, and recent experiments have shown that some natural latex can even deter insects.[8] Latex is generally odorless, which differentiates it from plant resins such as pine tar and copal incense that contain volatile oils, and thus strong aromas.[9]

The contemporary Maya refer to the sapodilla tree as *tzicte' ya'*, which I am roughly translating as "wounded noble tree." This is a descriptive name that reflects the way in which the latex is obtained. Chicleros (chicle extractors) harvest the chicle by cutting a machete into the flesh along the length of the tree in a zigzag pattern (fig. 1.1), and allowing the latex to run down the trunk.[10] Once the raw latex, or *itz* in Mayan, is collected, they then dry it and cook it. Cooking transforms the substance into what they call *cha*, which means that it is ready for chewing.[11] This is a process that the Maya have likely been using for hundreds, if not thousands of years, as the ancient Maya recognized that chewing this rubbery resin quenched thirst and staved off hunger.[12]

The Aztecs also chewed the chicle latex, which they referred to as *tzictli*. However, the term *tzictli* actually referred to two kinds of chewing gum. The tree latex was distinguished as "mountain chicle" or "wild" chicle and was considered to have a pleasing texture and a slightly sweet flavor. The other preferred chicle was made of bitumen, or *chapapote*, an aromatic and flaky black natural petroleum tar that washed up onto the beaches of the Gulf Coast of Mexico,[13] an area of major

Figure 1.1. A chiclero cutting a zigzag pattern into the sapodilla trunk for collecting chicle latex as he descends the tree. (Photograph courtesy of Macduff Everton)

oil drilling today. In some cases, Aztec women mixed the wild chicle and bitumen together to keep it from crumbling when it was chewed.[14] They would also soften the bitumen with axin, a yellowish oily substance that they obtained by cooking a small flylike insect and breaking open its shell. Although the bitumen had a more refreshing taste than the wild chicle, Spanish chronicler Fray Bernardino de Sahagún noted in his multivolume treatise on Aztec culture that when it is chewed, "[it] tires one's head; it gives one a headache."[15]

Spit Out Your Gum

Most people have been told by their parents or teachers at one time or another not to "smack your gum" or to "spit it out" and probably thought that this was a rule that a modern polite society developed. It is actually a social norm that has existed for gum chewers for centuries in the Americas. Among the Aztec, only unmarried women and young children were allowed to chew gum in public, while older women could only chew in private for sanitary reasons, such as to expel rheumatism,[16] or to rid bad mouth odor. As the dismayed narrator Sahagún explains:

> And the chewing of chicle [is] the preference, the privilege of little girls, the small girls, the young women. Also the mature women, the unmarried women use it; and all the women who [are] unmarried chew chicle in public. One's wife also chews chicle, but not in public. Also the widowed and the old women do not, in public. . . . For this reason the women chew chicle: because thereby they cause their saliva to flow and thereby the mouths are scented; the mouth is given a pleasing taste. With it they dispel the bad odor of their mouths, or the bad smell of their teeth. Thus they chew chicle in order not to be detested.[17]

Aztec norms strongly disparaged gum chewing among men, particularly in public. Sahagún continues in his chronicle:

> The men also chew chicle to cause their saliva to flow and to clean the teeth, but this very secretly—never in public. . . . The chewing of chicle [is] the real privilege of the addicts termed "effeminates." [It is] as if it were their privilege, their birthright. And the men who publicly chew chicle achieve the status of sodomites; they equal the effeminates.[18]

Figure 1.2. An image of the "Chicle Chewer" from the contact-period Florentine Codex that documents Aztec society (Sahagún 1979a:pl. 139). (Replica of the original 1590 manuscript; courtesy of la Biblioteca Medicea Laurenziana, Florence, Italy)

Aztec prostitutes were often identifiable by their sweet-smelling perfumes and the sound of gum smacking (fig. 1.2).[19] In the discussion by Sahagún of "the harlot, the carnal woman" in Aztec society, he states:

> She perfumes herself, casts incense about her, uses rose water. She uses the *poyomatli* herb. She chews chicle—she clacks chicle. She lives on the water—in the streets; she goes about disgracing the streets, frequenting the market place, as if part of the market place. . . . But the bad women, those called harlots, [show] no fine feelings; quite publicly they go about chewing chicle along the roads, in the market place, clacking like castanets. Other women who constantly chew chicle in public achieve the attributes of evil women.[20]

For the Aztecs, chewing chicle was a symbol of gender and sexual status, as the simple act of chewing gum in public identified a married or widowed woman as a whore and a male as a homosexual. This gender association with gum extended

Figure 1.3. The Mesoamerican goddess Tlazolteotl with bitumen tar around her mouth. (Photograph by Jennifer P. Mathews)

to their gods as well. The goddess Tlazolteotl, who was known as the "Great Spinner and Weaver," was the ultimate feminine being who was associated with childbirth, sexuality, healing, the moon, menstruation, and witchcraft. In another guise, she was known as the "filth eater," or Tlaelquanai, who ate a person's sins to absolve them before death. She was frequently portrayed with bitumen on her face and around her mouth (fig. 1.3), further emphasizing gum in general as a feminine symbol.[21]

Despite these stigmas, chicle seemed to be sold in the open market in Aztec society. Sahagún describes the small-scale merchant who sold rabbit hair, gourd bowls, dyes, pigments, red ochre, herbs, copal, bitumen, possum tail, wild chicle, and chicle mixed with bitumen (*tlaaxnelolli*)[22] in direct exchange for equally valuable items or the Mesoamerican currency of cacao (chocolate) beans. Besides being chewed, chicle served other purposes in ancient times. The ancient Maya sometimes mixed chicle and rubber with incense resin. For example, the copal remains dredged from the Cenote of Sacrifice at the site of Chichén Itzá in Yucatán, Mexico, were found wrapped in a layer of chicle and rubber. As chicle and rubber catch fire more easily than copal, researchers believe that the Maya did this to facilitate the burning of incense.[23] However, the Spanish bishop of Yucatán, Diego de Landa, also mentions in his sixteenth-century chronicles that chicle was sometimes used as incense in itself.[24] The artisans among the Coclé people of Panama even filled their gold ear rods with chicle latex. The gum served to hold separate pieces of goldwork together, as well as reinforced the thin sheets of gold from which the rods were made.[25] Undoubtedly ancient peoples utilized chicle latex for many practical purposes such as an adhesive or sealant, but chroniclers failed to document these uses.

The Sapodilla Tree: Ancient Use of Wood and Fruit

Sapodilla Wood

The sapodilla tree is highly resistant to drought and heat and is known for its extreme longevity. The ancient Maya, who referred to the tree as *ha'as*, prized the wood for its density and strength and used it widely, as many samples have been found in archaeological excavations. Whole seeds from the sapodilla tree have been found in middens at the ancient Maya sites of Colha in Belize and Tikal in Guatemala. Charcoal remains, presumably from firewood, have also been recovered at the Maya sites of Cuello, Wild Cane Caye, Pulltrouser Swamp, and Albion Island in Belize dating to the Preclassic (250 BC–AD 400) and Classic periods (AD 400–600).[26]

At the site of Palenque in Chiapas, the zapote tree is depicted on the renowned stone sarcophagus of the king Hanab-Pakal. The sides of the sarcophagus are illustrated with a series of ten figures, representing the ancestral royal family of Palenque. Each figure is shown wearing a headdress containing his or her name and associated with a valuable tree such as the avocado or cacao, representing an "orchard of the ancestors." Specifically, the image of K'an-Hok'-Chitam I shows the zapote tree emerging from behind him. The wood of the zapote tree was also used to make precious objects such as the unprovenanced carved sapodilla wood box known as the "Tortuguero Box," which measures 15.3 cm long and is rubbed with a layer of red hematite. Dating to the late seventh century AD, it is thought to have come from the Tortuguero region of Chiapas because it depicts a prominent lord known from a stela at Tortuguero. The box is covered with a narrative of forty-one Maya glyphs that likely describes the dynastic history of the ruler who owned it. Based on a similar plain box found in a cave in Belize, it probably contained bloodletting implements.[27] The reddish wood of the tree, more enduring than even mahogany, was also preferred for making roof beams and carved lintels at Maya sites like Chichén Itzá and Tikal (fig. 1.4).[28] The preservation of organic objects is rare in tropical climates, and Mesoamerican archaeology has greatly benefited from the durable quality of this wood.

The Aztecs also appreciated the hard quality of this wood, as Spanish chronicler Juan de Torquemada noted that when they made obsidian knives, workmen used hard wooden sticks to pressure-flake blades to prepare a core. Toolmakers would seat themselves with the stone core in their laps and push the end of the stick onto the edges of it to force the blades to flake off. Don Crabtree, a lithic replicator who experimented with various types of wood tools for creating blades, argued that they would have to have used an extremely tough wood like sapodilla for the sticks to hold up to this kind of work.[29] Outside observers documented that at the turn of the twentieth century, Maya hunters were using sapodilla wood to make arrows tipped with obsidian for hunting fish.[30] The sturdiness of this wood has made it a desirable resource for constructing the pole and thatch houses of Maya commoners for centuries. When clearing plots of land for agriculture, ancient Maya farmers doubtless left the sapodilla trees in the clearings because of their yields of wood, latex, and fruit.[31]

The ancient Maya are thought to have intentionally planted valuable trees like the sapodilla in specific areas of their cities so that the elite could maintain control of their yields. In a groundbreaking study, Folan, Fletcher, and Kintz tested the residence pattern of the ancient Maya city of Cobá in Quintana Roo, using Diego de Landa's sixteenth-century class-oriented description of Maya towns during pre-conquest times. Ancient Maya site planners shaped cities to reflect strong social class divisions as well as religious ideology. The center of site was the elite sector where rituals took place and the powerful families lived. Roads,

Figure 1.4. A reproduction of an original carved lintel made of sapodilla wood, from the Maya site of Tikal in Guatemala. (Photograph courtesy of Macduff Everton)

walls, and platforms acted as boundary markers for restricting access and defining ceremonial areas. The nonelite lived on the edges of the site center and maintained their kitchen gardens and fields that produced the majority of the city's food. In a survey that identified thousands of structures and trees across a central segment of the site, Folan and his colleagues observed the correlation between the location and quantity of certain trees producing fruit, fiber, bark, and resin and high-status vaulted architecture.[32]

At the center of the site of Cobá, near a series of lakes, there is a high concentration of elite vaulted architecture associated with fruit-, latex-, and resin-producing trees. Toward the fringes of the site, the rate of elite architecture drops dramatically, as does the presence of cultivated trees. Specifically, the latex- and resin-producing trees such as sapodilla and copal (used to make incense) were most concentrated

(72 percent) in the elite sector of Cobá. On the outskirts of Cobá, families had only approximately 18 percent of the latex-producing trees, which included only sapodilla and not copal. The authors speculate that this means that the elites would have controlled not only the products of these trees but also the associated ceremonial drinks, incense, and so on.[33] However, another possible hypothesis that explains this correlation of sapodilla trees with the site center is the interaction of bats with the sapodilla fruit. In addition to pollinating the sapodilla flower, bats prize the sweet fruit and automatically disperse the seeds where they eat them. They carry the whole fruits back to their roosts, which are commonly found in larger Maya ruins.[34] However, this does not explain the exclusive presence of the copal trees in the site center, and it is likely that there was at least some intentional planting and control of these valuable commodities by the elite.

Sapodilla Fruit

The sapodilla tree produces a sweet egg-shaped fruit known as "sapote" that was used as an ancient Maya and Aztec food source. The Spanish word *sapote* is corrupted from the Nahuatl term *tzapotl*, meaning "soft fruit," and thus was used to refer to soft fruits in general. The Maya, on the other hand, used the term *ya*, which specifically references the chicozapote fruit. The fruit has a brown skin much like a kiwi, a soft orange- or brown-colored flesh with a grainy texture and dark, smooth-skinned seeds.[35] After contact, the Spanish prized it for its sweetness and introduced it to the Old World (fig. 1.5). As was noted by Bishop Diego de Landa in his volume on Maya culture: "There is another very leafy and beautiful tree which never drops its leaves and without blossoming produces a fruit of as much and more sweetness than the one I have spoken of above, small, very sweet and delicious to eat and very delicate, and some are better than others and so much better that they would be highly prized if we had them here [in Spain]."[36] They also dried the fruit like prunes and were able to eat them year round, when other fruits were scarce.[37] Sapotes were also valued by the Nicarao peoples of Nicaragua. In Francisco Oviedo y Valdés's sixteenth-century chronicle of their culture, he noted that their currency of cacao (chocolate) beans had established values. A buyer could obtain eight sapota fruits at the cost of four cacao beans, while the company of a prostitute would run them about eight to

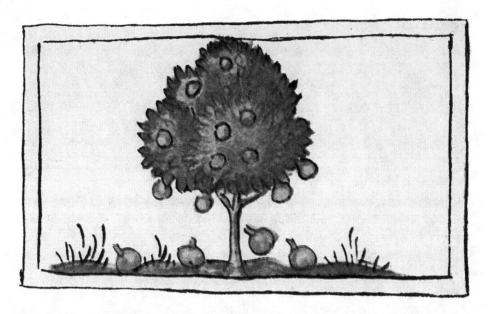

Figure 1.5. An image of a sapodilla tree from the Aztec-period Florentine codex (from Sahagún 1979b:pl. 311). (From a replica of the original 1590 manuscript; courtesy of la Biblioteca Medicea Laurenziana, Florence, Italy)

ten beans (depending on their negotiating skills), the purchase of a rabbit was ten beans, and a slave was worth one hundred.[38]

Fray Sahagún warned in his writings, however, that consumers of the fruit must be cautious of the seeds. "If much is eaten, it passes through one, it loosens the bowels, it gives one indigestion, it gives one diarrhea."[39] Nonetheless, the Aztecs used the sapote fruit seeds in their cuisine. Francisco Hernández, the royal physician and naturalist to Philip II of Spain, provides in his volume on the plants of New Spain a possible pre-contact Aztec recipe for "aphrodisiac" chocolate known as *chocolatl*. The recipe called for water to be mixed with equal parts of roasted cacao seeds, the heart of the sapodilla fruit seed, and dried maize, all ground and beaten into a frothy mixture. This would have been a fairly acrid drink, perhaps valued more for its supposed aphrodisiac qualities, because in addition to the bitterness of the chocolate beans, the sapodilla seeds have a bitter almond taste.[40]

Discussion

The sapodilla tree produces a wealth of natural products, including a latex that has been chewed in the Americas for centuries, a wood so durable that lintels from Classic-period Maya sites still exist, and a fruit that was worthy of bringing across the oceans to the Old World. Ancient peoples bled the sapodilla tree of its latex much like they did the copal tree, or *Bursera bipinnata* (DC.) Engl., to obtain copal resin, and the rubber tree or *Castilla elastica* (Sessé ex Cerv.) to collect rubber. Due to its similar characteristics to these natural by-products, ancient Mesoamericans may have seen chicle latex in a comparable light—a valuable good that served both ritual and practical purposes. Although we might assume that artifacts and ecofacts (natural objects that are not modified by humans but tell us something about human behavior) fall neatly into utilitarian or ritual categories, Hodder argues that most artifacts (and presumably ecofacts) had flexible uses and could serve domestic and ceremonial purposes within their life spans.[41] Similarly, prehistoric peoples could employ and value botanical products such as resins and latexes for their practical and ceremonial purposes.[42] The ancient Mesoamerican perception of the landscape and the objects within it was multilayered and complex, and the same object or material such as copal, rubber, or chicle could serve multiple purposes.

The ancient Maya burned copal in lump form in various types of wood, gourd, or ceramic incense burners, just as it is used today (fig. 1.6). When copal was burned, the smoke rose to the sky and provided a kind of sustenance for their deities—a "food of the gods."[43] The gods were also thought to come down to receive these offerings, which may explain "diving god" figures (fig. 1.7) found with balls of copal in their hands.[44] However, copal resin also served practical purposes. Ancient Maya artisans used a thin layer of copal to adhere cinnabar to greenstone objects and as a binder for the paint pigments used in the well-known murals at the site of Bonampak in Chiapas.[45] The resin was also used medicinally in pre-contact and colonial Yucatán to "warm the body" and to help cure headaches.[46] The contemporary Zinancantan Maya even use it to reinforce loose teeth and plug cavities, while the Chortí Maya use the resin to treat stomachaches, nosebleeds, fevers, headaches, and burns, and as a wood glue and a repellent for bugs.[47]

Rubber latex was also a valuable commodity to ancient Mesoamericans that served multiple purposes. Numerous cultural groups including the Olmec, Maya,

Figure 1.6. Incense being burned by a modern shaman in Yucatán. (Photograph courtesy of Macduff Everton)

Figure 1.7. A detail of the Diving God, possibly holding a ball of copal, at the Maya site of Tulum in Quintana Roo. (Photograph courtesy of Macduff Everton)

and Aztec used rubber to produce balls for the ritual ballgame, as well as for creat-ing human figurines and body parts as sacrificial offerings. Archaeologists even dredged up a human skull incense burner with burned red rubber on the interior in Chichén Itzá's Cenote of Sacrifice.[48] The chronicler Diego de Landa recorded that the Maya used rubber on the tips of drumsticks, which was likely preferred for the sound it produced while beating drums made of hollow logs.[49] Ancient peoples valued rubber for its water-proofing qualities,[50] and Fray Bernardino de Sahagún reported that the Aztecs even used it on the soles of sandals,[51] probably to make them last longer and provide traction. The Aztecs also utilized rubber latex for its medicinal properties, including rubber drops that were put down the throat for curing hoarseness. Rubber could also be formed into suppositories to help with colic, urinary problems in males, and fertility issues in females, and mixed with cacao, water, and chiles (likely to improve the taste) to help with ailments such as "spitting of blood." They also applied liquid rubber to ulcers in the ear, mixed with salt to the interior of the nostrils to cure dryness, and directly to lip sores. Roys observed that the Maya used rubber to treat hemorrhoids, and in a potion form to treat dysentery. Among the modern Huastec, rubber is dried and used for headaches and toothaches.[52]

Ancient Mesoamericans saw copal and rubber as the "blood of the tree" and used it as a primary ingredient for creating offerings to their gods, as well as for everyday uses. It is quite likely that they similarly viewed chicle latex as a natural product that could serve ritual and practical purposes. While it was certainly not traded as widely nor was it as prevalent in ritual settings as copal and rubber, we know that the Maya have used chicle as a kind of incense, as well as wrapped it on the outside of ritual copal offerings. While some may argue that chicle serves a more utilitarian purpose (i.e., as a chewing gum, a sealant, and an additive that helps copal to burn easier), it seems that is a simplification of its use. The Maya often mixed objects such as jade beads, shell, rubber, maize, and cacao with copal,[53] or even shaped rubber and copal resin into objects such as ears of corn[54] or animal hearts.[55] This conflation of the objects that could be both sacred and mundane was completely intentional and reflected their complex view of the natural world. Chicle latex would have similarly crossed the boundaries and served multiple aims.

2

THE BOTANY OF THE SAPODILLA TREE

"That is one crazy tree!"
—Conclusion reached by a botanist after extensive research on the sapodilla

The sapodilla is a tree of contradictions, and sometimes it is not even a tree. In the wild, it is found in a range of habitats from coastal sand dunes and seasonally inundated swamps (*tintales*) to mature old-growth tropical forest. It can be found growing as a mature spindly shrub or a tree that reaches 45 m (147 ft) tall. It is reported to tolerate soil salinity at levels seen only in date palms (*Phoenix dactylifera L.*). While it is a protected species in Mexico, it is considered to be an invasive tree in the state of Florida. In its native Mesoamerica, the species is valued for its latex, while the rest of the world prizes more than fifty cultivars (plant varieties selected and cultivated by humans because of particular attributes) for their fruit. This chapter will explore the natural history of the sapodilla and its remarkable adaptability to nature and the human hand.

Nomenclature and Taxonomy

There are many species still exploited for their latex in the American tropics; among them are several related species belonging to the genus *Manilkara*, including *Manilkara zapota* (L.) P. Royen, *Manilkara chicle* (Pittier) Gilly, *Manilkara staminodella* Gilly, and *Manilkara bidentata* (A. DC.) A. Chev.[1] The preferred source of chicle is *Manilkara zapota*, although these relatives and other species were sometimes tapped and their milky saps used to adulterate the "true" chicle.[2] While it is not difficult to differentiate the sapodilla from its relatives in the field, confusion nonetheless abounds within the literature. Much of this confusion has arisen from the messy nomenclature that has plagued the sapodilla since Carolus

Linnaeus first published the species description in 1753 in *Species Plantarum* (vol. 2). Linnaeus created these volumes as an attempt to synthesize all animal and plant species known at the time, and worked with whatever materials were available. Because Linnaeus seldom left his native Sweden, he relied on his students who traveled and brought back many of the specimens upon which he worked. He also based many of his eight thousand plant descriptions on the drawings and verbal descriptions of earlier explorers, some of whom were dead and could not be consulted. Occasionally, inaccuracies or contradictory information in the available resources led to incorrect species designations, as was the case with sapodilla.

Linnaeus originally designated the species *Achras sapota* L. based upon both unpublished descriptions and published drawings by the French botanist Charles Plumier[3] in his volume *Nova Plantarum Americanarum Genera*. Plumier used the term "sapota" for two types of fruit but never published full textual descriptions to explain how they differed.[4] To this ambiguity, Plumier added confusion by his illustrations of the flowers, which were inaccurate in their representation of both the number and arrangement of the sepals (a modified leaf that collectively forms the calyx that protects the interior of a flower).[5] Linnaeus based his description of *Achras sapota* on both the drawings of Plumier and those of another botanist, Hans Sloane, a Scotsman who had collected in the West Indies and Jamaica in the late eighteenth century. Linnaeus's designation of *Achras sapota* was further complicated because Plumier's illustrations were examples of two variations he saw in the sapodilla, while the Sloane illustrations were actually of a separate species in an entirely different genus known as *Pouteria sapota* (Jacq.) Moore and Stearn.[6]

This nomenclatural confusion continued, as taxonomist after taxonomist persisted in interpreting the natural variability of the one species as many species, well into the twentieth century.[7] The result is that more than fifty scientific synonyms show up in the literature, with most of these based upon slight differences in the floral structure. In the 1990 revision of the species for *Flora Neotropica*,[8] Pennington rejects these floral differences as nondiagnostic.[9] Moore and Stearn attempted to lay the issue to rest and proclaimed *Manilkara zapota* as the accepted taxonomic name, though the more familiar synonyms appear in the literature to this day.[10]

In the American horticultural literature, researchers refer to the species as sapodilla, but there are also a number of common names for *Manilkara zapota*, ranging from "chikoo" in India, to "dilly" in the Bahamas and British West Indies, "lamoot" in Thailand, and "naseberry" in Jamaica.[11] Even more misunderstandings arise because many of the common names are applied to other plant species. For example, "sapodilla" and "sapote" (zapote) are also used for *Diospyros digyna* Jacq. (black sapote), *Pouteria sapota* (Jacq.) Moore and Stearn (mamey sapote), *Pouteria campechiana* (Kunth) Baehni (canistel, or eggfruit tree), and *Casimiroa edulis* Llave and Lex (white sapote). There is no current resolution to the preponderance of scientific and common names, but as the chewing gum industry obtained its supply from the *M. zapota*, and sapodilla is the most widespread common name used in the literature for this species, this is the common name we have chosen to use.

Distribution and Uses of Sapodilla

Manilkara zapota is one of fifty-five or so species that make up the genus *Manilkara* found in tropical and subtropical areas of the Americas, Asia, and Africa. Of the thirty species found in the New World, *M. zapota* is arguably the most economically important, producing fruit, latex, and lumber. Other members of the genus are exploited to a lesser extent; *Manilkara chicle* is used for its latex and fruit, while *Manilkara staminodella* is used only for its latex. In South America, *Manilkara bidentata* is used to produce chewing gum, lumber, and fruit, while in Central America and the West Indies it is employed for an array of products ranging from electrical and marine cable insulation to golf ball coverings and root canal fillings.[12] As *Manilkara zapota*, *M. chicle*, and *M. staminodella* all have overlapping geographic ranges, and all three were tapped for chicle, it is likely that Mesoamerican chicleros adulterated the *M. zapota* latex with the latter two species. These are both considered to produce latex of an inferior quality, and *Manilkara staminodella* even has the common name "chicle de segunda"—or second-rate chicle.[13]

The sapodilla tree is a slow-growing evergreen native to the tropical evergreen (*selva alta perennifolia*) and semideciduous (*selva alta subperennifolia, selva mediana*) forests of Mesoamerica, including the Mexican states of Veracruz, Oaxaca, Chiapas, Quintana Roo, and Campeche, the Alta Verapaz and Petén regions of Guatemala, northern Belize, and the Atlantic coastal forests of Nicaragua (fig. 2.1).[14] In many of these forests, *M. zapota* is a dominant or codominant

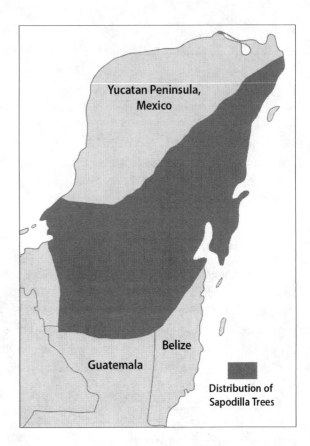

Figure 2.1. The natural distribution of the sapodilla tree in Mesoamerica. (Map by Jennifer P. Mathews, after Hodge 1955:77)

species, and is often seen growing in association with *Brosimum alicastrum* Swartz (*ramón*), *Swietenia macrophylla King.* (*caoba*, mahogany), and *Terminalia amazonia* (*guayabo*)(J. F. Gmel.) Exell. This is also one of the few tree species found in coastal-dune vegetation on the Yucatán Peninsula and in seasonal wetlands in both southeastern and western Mexico.[15]

Physical Traits of the Sapodilla

Older trees are easily identified by the diagonal scars that run the length of their trunks indicating that the tree was tapped for latex (fig. 2.2). The tree has a dense

Figure 2.2. A detail of a chiclero cutting the bark of a sapodilla tree to obtain latex. (Photograph courtesy of Macduff Everton)

canopy with a rounded or pyramidal shape that can spread up to 12 m (40 ft) across. While young branches are covered with loose brown hairs, the bark becomes smooth as the branches age. Mature trees have a bark that ranges from dark brown to gray and is deeply fissured and cracked. When slashed, the inner bark is pink and exudes the sticky white latex. Another distinctive feature of the sapodilla is sympodial branching, a growth pattern in which the main axis of the plant is made up of many lateral branches.[16] The leaves are spirally arranged and clustered at the tips of these branches. They are usually dark green in color, leathery in texture, and have a glossy surface (fig. 2.3). The leaf has an elliptic to oblong shape with pointed ends and ranges in size from 6.6 to 11 cm (2.5–5.7 in.) and 2 to 5.2 cm (1–2.4 in.), though some of the cultivars have larger leaves. The venation (arrangement of the vascular tissue) on the leaves is usually a distinctive yellow color, with the lateral veins joining the midrib almost at right angles. When plucked from a branch, the leaves will produce a small amount of latex as a way of protecting the tree from damage by insects or herbivores. This characteristic encouraged the chicle industry to make a minor attempt to increase yields in the 1930s by extracting latex from the leaves, but they produced so little that the experiment was abandoned.[17]

The inconspicuous flowers are bell shaped, white to greenish in color, and are found in the axils (the point at which the leaf joins the stem) of the leaves. They have a sweet scent and are found either singly or in dense clusters on the branches. The individual flower consists of six fused petals surrounded by two whorls of three sepals each. The outer whorl is covered with short brown hairs, similar to the hairs found on young branches. Inside the corolla are six stamens (the male organ) and also six petal-like staminodes (rudimentary stamens that are sterile and, in the case of sapodilla, are petal-like in form) that alternate with the petals (fig. 2.4). Sapodillas produce flowers in flushes throughout the year in their natural range.[18]

The fruit, commonly known as sapota, is a berry that can grow up to 10 cm in diameter (4 in.) and varies in shape from round to elliptical (see fig. 2.3). The fuzzy, sandy-brown skin surrounds a sweet yellow, orange, or brownish pulp that can be creamy or gritty in texture and extremely sweet at the peak of ripeness. Its perfume, flavor, and texture are often compared to that of a ripe pear. Prior to maturing, the fruits are unpalatable, as they are filled with latex, and are astringent due to a high concentration of tannins. Tannins are also responsible for the astringent (mouth-puckering) quality of tea, wine, and some fruits, including cranberries and pomegranates.[19] The wild fruits contain between two and twelve black seeds, though some cultivated species are seedless.[20]

Ecology and Reproduction

Manilkara zapota tolerates a wide variety of environmental conditions. In its natural range, the species grows in soils that vary from the almost pure limestone soils

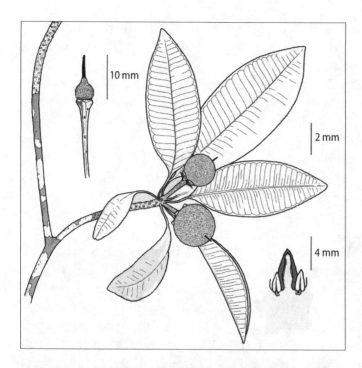

Figure 2.3 The *Manilkara zapota*, including the pistil and internal flower morphology (petal, staminode, and stamens). (Original drawing courtesy of Mitchell C. Provance)

Figure 2.4. The flower of the *Manilkara zapota*. (Photograph courtesy of Gerald D. Carr)

of the Yucatán Peninsula to the sandy soils found in coastal areas. In cultivation, it thrives in medium-textured loams as well as in heavy clays with marginal drainage.[21] The species is drought tolerant, but can also withstand prolonged periods of saturation. Several studies have demonstrated a marked tolerance to root-zone salinity, rivaling that of the date palm, which is the world's most salt-tolerant tree fruit crop.[22] The only major limitation to the distribution of this tree appears to be temperature: prolonged nighttime temperatures below −3°C (27°F) and/or daytime temperatures that reach above 42°C (107°F) can stunt or kill young trees. While mature adult trees can withstand temperatures below freezing for short periods, young trees are killed by even just a few nights of frost.[23] Although the tree has been cultivated at elevations up to 1,000 m (3,280 ft) in India, it is limited to only 800 m (2,624 ft) in Mesoamerica.[24]

The process of plant reproduction takes place in the flowers. In some species, the flowers are unisexual, with only stamens or carpels but not both. In most flowering plant species such as the sapodilla, the flowers are bisexual and have both stamens and carpels. In either case, plant reproduction involves two steps: pollination and fertilization. A typical flower contains a combination of four types of organs: sepals, petals, stamens, and carpels. When present, the sepals and petals are the attention-getters that attract a pollinator to a plant. The stamens, made up of a stalk called a filament and a head called an anther, are more practical in purpose and produce the plant's sperm within the protective shell of a pollen grain. The flower's female organs, or carpels, consist of three parts: a stigma, style, and ovary. The stigma and style receive the pollen and then in the process of pollination transmit it to the egg, which is produced in the ovary. If the pollen is from the right species and genetically compatible, it germinates on the stigma and sends a pollen tube down to the ovary through which the sperm will travel and complete the second part of the process—fertilization. If fertilization is successful, the embryo will eventually develop into a seed within the ovary of the flower. If a pollen grain is not compatible with the stigma, germination and fertilization will fail.

Much of the diversity that we see in flowers today has evolved in response to plants trying to get their pollen to the right stigma. Some plants are autogamous, or capable of self-fertilization, because pollen can successfully fertilize the eggs within the same flower. However, as one of the primary goals of sexual reproduction is to increase variability in a species by combining genetic material from two different individuals, many plants have evolved mechanisms that prevent "selfing" (self-propagation) from occurring. Those plants, known as outcrossers, must find some way to transfer their pollen to another flower entirely. This process could be as simple as moving the pollen between flowers on the same plant (geitonogamy), but most species prefer that their pollen be moved to a different individual entirely (obligate outcrossers). There are a multitude of methods to achieve pollination. Some plants use wind, which due to its imprecise nature requires the production of huge amounts of pollen in the hopes of a few grains finding their mark. Other plants, either through trickery or reward, have found ways to entice animals to carry the pollen from one flower to another. It is this smarter strategy that prevails in most tropical forest tree species, including the sapodilla.

Only a few scholars have studied the reproductive biology of the sapodilla, and the results vary depending on the study. An examination of cultivated sapodilla in Florida demonstrated that cross-pollination was significantly more successful than self-pollination. Of sixty-four self-pollinations, none set fruit, while cross-pollinated trees set fruit in 10 percent to 100 percent of cases. In India,[25] however, another study found that at least some cultivated sapodilla trees do successfully self-pollinate with the aid of slow and timid insects known as thrips who feed on the pollen grains as well as nectar and other exudates produced in the flowers.[26] The author noted that the two diminutive thrips species (*Thrips hawaiiensis* and *Haplothrips tenuipennis*) commonly present were unable to fly very far and thus often only transferred pollen between flowers on the same tree.[27]

The few studies that have examined the breeding biology of wild sapodilla indicate that it is an obligate outcrosser.[28] The sapodilla is an abundant species in older forests throughout its native range and can reach densities as high as eighty-five trees per hectare,[29] though lower densities are more common. Several authors have noted a high concentration of sapodillas around archaeological sites and have suggested that ancient populations may have planted or encouraged these trees.[30] Other recent studies of sapodilla seeds[31] and seedling demography[32] suggest that the species' biology may also contribute to this distribution.

Although little research has focused on the pollinator(s) of wild sapodilla, what evidence there is indicates that bats, including *Carollia perspicillata* (short-tailed bats) and various members of the genus *Artibeus*, are frequent visitors.[33] The configuration of the sapodilla tree suits bats, because they favor flowers that are typically white or cream colored and have a sweet or musky scent, and are arranged in clumps that hang below the foliage allowing them to navigate between them in the dark.[34] Bats that visit sapodilla flowers are rewarded with protein-rich pollen, small amounts of nectar, and the flesh of the flowers themselves. While bats are feeding, the fur on their heads and necks inadvertently becomes dusted with pollen, which they may transfer to the stigma of the next flowers they visit. Because bats move constantly while foraging each night, they are able to travel between 400 m (~1,300 ft) and 38 km (~23.6 mi) a day. This kind of long-distance pollination increases the likelihood that they will fertilize an unrelated individual and consequently improve the population's genetic diversity.[35]

Once fertilization has occurred and the fruits have developed, the next challenge for a parent plant is to move their offspring away. This has two benefits: first, it increases the size and range of the species' distribution, and second, it decreases potential competition between the parent and offspring for water and nutrients. Many plant species have evolved fruits that tempt particular animals through color, smell, texture, and size. The animal eats the fruit, often after carrying it some distance from the tree, and then either spits out or passes the seeds though its gut, "releasing" them with a pile of fertilizer. The sweet sapota fruit attracts many different species of animals to the trees, including parrots (*Amazona* spp.), howler monkeys (*Aloutta* spp.), spider monkeys (*Ateles* spp.), and most importantly bats.[36]

Multiple bat species consume sapodilla fruit, including the Jamaican fruit-eating bat (*Artibeus jamaicensis*), the Trinidadian fruit bat (*A. lituratus*), and Seba's short-tailed bat (*Carollia perspicillata*).[37] The Caribbean fruit bat (*Artibeus jamaicensis parvipes*) has been observed roosting in stands of sapodilla trees in Cuba[38] and the Yucatán Peninsula.[39] As archaeological sites in Mesoamerica have an abundance of bats and sapodilla trees, one botanist suggests that this distribution may be the result of bats dispersing the fruit, rather than strictly human activities.[40] Once the fruits fall to the ground, animals such as kinkajous (*Potos flavus*), tapirs (*Tapirus bairdii*), and peccaries (*Pecari* sp.) snatch them up.[41] In Florida, naturalized populations of sapodilla are dispersed by raccoons (*Procyon lotor*), opossums (*Didelphis virginiana*), and key deer (*Odocoileus virginianus*).[42]

When the seeds hit the soil in the forest, a mad race is on for the seeds to germinate and the seedlings to outgrow all other plants for light, nutrients, and resources. A high number of tree stems growing in a forest can make it particularly difficult for young plants to grow. In tropical rain forests, stem densities can range between 320 and 600 stems (measuring 10 cm, or 4 in.) per ha (hectare) dbh (diameter at breast height).[43] When smaller stem sizes are included in forest structure studies, densities can approach 6,000 stems/ha, creating a particularly challenging growth environment.[44] Plants have evolved different strategies to overcome this challenge: some species maintain seed banks, while others maintain seedling banks. Seed banks are large numbers of dormant seeds in the soil that are waiting for just the right set of environmental conditions so that they can explode out of the soil and grow up toward the light. A fallen tree or even a fallen branch could create just such a light gap, providing a window in the dense canopy that admits the light and warmth necessary for germination.[45]

A major problem with this strategy is that seeds might be eaten by hungry animals or digested by fungi and bacteria while waiting for perfect conditions. The seed bank strategy is not an option for the sapodilla tree since the seeds are classified as recalcitrant or intermediate,[46] meaning that they usually germinate quickly or not at all; they do not tolerate dormancy, desiccation, or low temperatures. Because sapodilla seeds are difficult to store for any period of time, horticulturalists frequently report that the tree is tricky to propagate from seed.[47] The ability to germinate quickly prevents seed predation from rodents and fungi. Quick germination also helps sapodilla seedlings avoid both intraspecific (within species) and interspecific (between species) competition for light and resources in tropical forests. Fast sprouters dominate slower species in this hypercompetitive environment.

While the sapodilla does not maintain seed banks, it does maintain seedling banks that often carpet the forest floor, creating a seedling shadow near parent trees. The seedlings are shade tolerant and the cotyledons (seed leaves) persist for up to eight months, allowing the seedling to carry out photosynthesis before expending energy to produce true leaves. A two-year study by Cruz-Rodríguez and López Mata found that seedling survival appeared to be very high (> 82 percent), and was strongly correlated with the size and number of leaves produced. The seedlings also had little evidence of physical damage from insects or other predators, something the authors attribute to the protective presence of latex.[48] The sapodilla appears to be a gap-dependent species, meaning that the seedlings grow slowly until a disturbance forms an opening in the canopy, at which point they grow rapidly to take advantage of the light.[49]

Sapodilla is extremely resilient in the face of disturbance. In 1984, a group of American and Mexican ecologists set out to understand the forest dynamics in a patch of dry tropical forest in northeastern Quintana Roo, Mexico. In September 1988, their research plots took a direct hit from Hurricane Gilbert, the second most intense hurricane in the Western Hemisphere (surpassed only by Wilma in 2005).[50] Gilbert had peak winds of 295 km per hour (185 mph) and was rated a category 5 on the Saffir-Simpson scale, leading the researchers to expect heavy damage. Approximately one month after the hurricane, they returned to assess the forest changes and were surprised to find many of the trees still standing and a relatively low overall mortality. This research revealed that tree species in the Yucatán Peninsula, including sapodilla, exhibited fairly quick recovery from the damage, and though under normal conditions trees exhibited a slow growth rate, after the disturbance the rate increased to above the pre-hurricane mean.[51]

Cultivars and Cultivation

Although wild sapodilla trees have been harvested for a combination of their latex, wood, and fruit, small-scale cultivation of the trees has developed almost exclusively for the fruit. Spanish colonists, who spoke so highly of the sapota in their writings, first brought the tree to the Philippines and Thailand in the sixteenth century. From there the species spread throughout southeast Asia, reaching Ceylon by 1802.[52] As a slow-growing and slow-to-reproduce species, plantation owners found it to be an unsuitable crop.[53] Researchers working for chewing gum companies also discovered that these domesticated sapodillas yielded low flows of latex and thus cultivation was not in the industry's best interest. This may have been because the cultivars had been originally chosen for their fruit quality, and in the selection process other qualities, such as latex production, decreased.

Today the sapodilla is cultivated on a small scale in the Philippines,[54] Thailand, Malaysia, Vietnam, Mexico, Puerto Rico, Venezuela,[55] the West Indies, Florida,[56] and California[57] and on plantations in India.[58] Researchers do not know if these cultivars are different species, as there is little interaction between growers from different regions.[59] We do know that most cultivars are selected primarily for different qualities of the fruit, including size, shape, color, taste, periodicity, and seed number, though in Florida the sapodilla is primarily grown as an ornamental tree.[60]

Outside of its native range, sapodilla is usually propagated asexually, due to both the variability in seed set (the percentage number of seeds that actually germinate) and because of the relatively lengthy amount of time (six to ten years) between planting and fruit production.[61] Unlike many fruit trees, the sapodilla seeds do not grow true to the cultivar of origin. If ten seeds from a single sapodilla fruit germinate, the resulting ten trees can vary radically in height, shape, production of fruit, and in the size, coloration, and taste of the fruit. Growers ensure consistent trees and fruit quality by asexual reproduction, which means, essentially, cloning.[62] Asexual reproduction is done by grafting or layering techniques and more recently micropropagation (see below). The main advantage for using asexual reproductive techniques is that the tree's ability to produce fruit will occur in three to five years as opposed to the usual six to ten mentioned above.[63]

Grafting involves the joining of the stem of one plant (called a scion) to a rooted portion of another plant (called a stock or rootstock). Scions from early-maturing trees guarantee early fruit production, and they can be grafted to root systems that are adapted to a particular climate or soil type. Grafting also helps to replicate pest-resistant strains and sought-after dwarf varieties. Dwarfing is particularly important with sapodilla cultivation because *M. zapota* can attain heights of 20 m (65.61 ft) or more, which makes the harvesting of the fruit more difficult.[64] Grafting techniques used with sapodilla include veneer grafting, cleft grafting, tongue grafting, whip grafting, side inarching, and saddle grafting.[65] These selective cloning techniques have led to the development of over 23,000 ha of plantations in central and southern India where the fruit is considered a delicacy.[66]

Another method of asexual reproduction used for sapodilla is layering. Generally, layering involves allowing branches to form roots while still attached to the parent plant. The rooted shoot is then removed and transplanted in a growing medium (usually soil, perlite, or agar). While there are a number of layering methods, the most commonly used for sapodilla is air layering.[67] Air layering is a process in which the cambium (vascular tissue in woody plants that translocates sugars) is girdled. The girdled or cut cambium is wrapped with water-holding material such as soaked cloth, cotton batting, or sphagnum moss, and the new roots seek the moisture. Once new roots have formed, the branch is removed from the parent plant and transplanted either to a pot or directly into the ground. When growers add plant growth hormones, it greatly enhances the success of propagation.[68]

While veneer grafting and air layering are the most commonly used methods of propagation, both have been criticized because of the relatively low success rate and/or the time it takes for the plants to become established.[69] A recent study by Purohit and Singhvi argues that micropropagation might be a faster method. In their research, they produced 500 seedlings through micropropagation, 444 of which were successfully transplanted after one year. Growing cells or tissues scraped from a desired plant are placed in a solution containing nutrients and specific plant hormones that encourage root and shoot formation. Most plant cells are totipotent (unspecialized) and with the correct stimulus can become any type of specialized plant cell (pluripotent) or even grow into an entire plant.[70] Thus micropropagation is a useful method for ensuring true-to-type clones and is already widely used for cloning a variety of economically important species such as potatoes, sugarcane, bananas, lilies, and orchids.[71]

Although the local environmental conditions dictate specific watering and fertilizer regimes, once sapodilla seedlings are established they require relatively little care. As a drought-tolerant species, only young trees require frequent irrigation, though regular watering can increase fruit yield in older trees.[72] While sapodilla does not require heavy inputs of fertilizer, the quantity and quality of the fruit crop increase with the addition of nitrogen, phosphorus, and particularly potassium.[73] When compared to other tropical fruit species, cultivated sapodilla is relatively pest-free and generally suffers from insect pests only in poorly managed orchards.[74] Sapodilla is also remarkably disease-free, though some cultivars are more susceptible than others.[75]

The greatest challenges of commercial sapodilla fruit production revolve around erratic production and storage after harvest. While sapodilla typically produces many flowers, the majority do not set fruit unless cultivators use hand pollination to cross-pollinate.[76] Higher fruit set also occurs when cross-pollination takes place between trees of the same cultivar, suggesting that at least some cultivars are incompatible with each other.[77] One study showed that only 1.6 percent of an individual tree's flowers fully developed into fruit.[78] Following fruit set, substantial fruit drop occurs. For the remaining fruits, maturation takes between four and ten months, and there are two growth periods. Immature fruits are astringent and full of latex, so harvest at full maturity is critical. While fruits can be harvested after the first growth period, the size and quality is enhanced if they are allowed to complete the second stage, during which sugar content increases.[79] Mature fruits can be easily identified because they shed their scruffy brown outer layer, leaving them with a smooth corky-brown surface with a yellow tinge. Other maturity indicators include fruit width and length and the absence of latex when the surface is lightly scratched.[80] Despite these markers, large-scale harvesting is not a possibility because fruits on the same tree and even those within the same cluster will mature at different times.[81]

Sapodilla fruit, like the banana, is climacteric, meaning that it continues to ripen following harvest. This ripening occurs quickly, and the fruits must be consumed within 8–10 days or spoilage will cause them to be inedible.[82] It is for this reason that most of the sapota is consumed fresh as a dessert fruit or is used in making ice cream. Growers have attempted to prolong shelf life using cold storage and growth-retarding chemicals such as ethylene, but these substantially affect the fruit quality.[83] Processing such as canning, dehydration, and freezing causes the fruit to lose much of its character and has not caught on.[84] The sum of these factors has greatly limited expansion of the commercial market in India[85] and elsewhere.

Medicinal Uses of Sapodilla

The medicinal uses are wide ranging for sapodilla, though it does not play a large role in the ethnopharmacology of the contemporary peoples in its native range. In Central America, the Lacandón Maya of Chiapas use bark of sapodilla for stomach pain, and rub the bark on the gums to treat toothaches and headaches.[86] The Yucatec Maya are reported to use decoctions (teas produced from the coarse parts of the plant such as bark, roots, and stems) of the leaves and bark to treat fever, gastrointestinal disorders, and pain and the latex for parasites and worms.[87] A fluid extracted from the crushed seeds is reportedly used in the Yucatán as a sedative and sleep aid, and a combined decoction of sapodilla and chayote (*Cnidoscolus acotinifolius*) leaves is used to reduce blood pressure. People living in the tropics also use the latex as a crude filling for tooth cavities,[88] a technique used for centuries.

Researchers have reported that folk uses have developed in areas where travelers introduced the sapodilla after contact. In Trinidad and Tobago, locals dry and ground the seeds into a paste and apply it to wounds on dogs to prevent and treat myiasis, a condition in which fly larvae feed on the tissues of their host.[89] Lans suggests that this is possibly derived from a similar human remedy used against the chiggoe flea (*Tunga penetrans* Linn.), and on stings and bites from venomous animals. They also use the crushed seeds to expel bladder and kidney stones, as they have a diuretic effect.[90]

Researchers conducting chemical analyses of sapodilla have confirmed the presence of several pharmacologically active compounds in sapodilla by-products, including saponins and sapotonins.[91] Saponins are organic compounds found widely in plants and a few marine animals such as sea cucumbers and sea stars. The name refers to their tendency to form a soapy foam when agitated in water, and many plants that are rich in saponin are used as natural detergents. It is likely that plants produce saponins as a chemical defense against microbial activity. Several studies indicate that the sapogenins are responsible for the sapodilla wood's resistance to termite and microbial damage[92] and are at least partially responsible for the durability of sapodilla wood carvings at archaeological sites.[93] As pharmacological agents, saponins exhibit anti-inflammatory, anticoagulant, antibacterial, and antifungal properties, as well as have the ability to stimulate the immune system.[94]

Laboratory investigations into the chemical activity of the sapodilla bark and fruit have also found the presence of anthocyanins and a number of phenolic compounds, including tannins.[95] Anthocyanins and tannins are thought to behave as antioxidants in the sapodilla's fruits, seeds, and bark.[96] Antioxidants are chemical compounds that play a protective role in living things by neutralizing free radicals (chemicals with unpaired electrons) that are produced during the process of oxidation. Medical researchers are interested in identifying plant sources of antioxidants, as they have been demonstrated to prevent and slow the progression of chronic diseases such as cancer and cardiovascular disease, as well as the decline in immune function and neurogenerative disorders. Plants probably produce tannins to deter insect and ruminant herbivory (hoofed plant-eating animals with four-chambered stomachs such as deer), as they bind to the plant's proteins, making them indigestible or even toxic to the consumer.[97] In sapodilla, tannins (and other antioxidants) have the highest concentration in unripe fruits, and decline as the fruits ripen though they are still found at levels comparable to the blueberry, a fruit that is used as a benchmark for antioxidant activity.[98] One laboratory study of the sapota isolated antioxidants that had a toxic effect on colon cancer cell lines.[99] These findings demonstrate the potential importance of continued study of the sapodilla and its by-products.

Discussion

Throughout the forests of Mesoamerica, the sapodilla still bears the scars of its usefulness. Understanding the botanical characteristics of this tree helps explain why humans have valued it and its natural by-products for centuries. Its adaptability to various climatic and environmental conditions makes it a hearty species and has allowed growers to introduce it in a variety of locations. The sapota fruit is appealing for its sweetness and its medicinal attributes. The tree's defensive traits, such as the latex exudate and its antimicrobial properties, result in products such as a handy elastic gum and a durable wood. These qualities, which have helped this species to adapt so effectively to its environment, have also made it a target for human exploitation. Although the tree has withstood this mistreatment and continues to thrive in forests around the world, many were casualties of the chicle industry in the nineteenth and twentieth centuries. Many immature trees were tapped too early, and mature trees were tapped too often, by untrained chicleros or those chicleros who had no thought for the future.

3

THE HISTORY OF THE CHEWING GUM INDUSTRY IN THE AMERICAS

> I know that I have contributed to the Building of that Home more than any one living. I have not only made Chewing Gum a pastime, but I have made it an Art. I have brought it right out in Public and Chewed before some of the oldest Political Families of Massachusetts.
> —Humorist Will Rogers, the most famous gum chewer of his time, after he was refused entrance to William Wrigley Jr.'s mansion on Catalina Island[1]

> This will never be a civilized country until we spend more money for books than we do chewing gum.
> —Writer and editor Elbert Hubbard, commenting about society in the United States during the early twentieth century[2]

The story of chicle chewing gum reaches its pinnacle during the development of chicle as an industry in the United States and Mesoamerica. It involves the growth of the major gum corporations in the United States and their subsequent impact on the countries where chicle was extracted. The large-scale commercial promise of chicle was not realized until the late 1800s, despite the fact that the Maya and Aztec had used it as a boutique product for centuries.[3] During the late nineteenth and twentieth centuries, laborers extracted chicle for an emerging chewing gum industry that was filled with fascinating characters and intriguing tales. The rapid growth of this business produced a uniquely American innovation that has endured over a century, created several U.S. millionaires and thousands of jobs across the Americas. Like the boom-and-bust industry of numerous extractive commodities, however, it greatly impacted the economies, forests, and people where chicle was found. After the fall of the natural chicle gum industry, synthetic chewing gum filled its void and new products have continued to evolve and expand. Today, chicle is once again being extracted on a small scale for an emerging boutique natural gum industry.

Prehistoric Chewing Gums

Chicle has a long tradition in the Americas that has bridged thousands of years. However, much like the first commercial chewing gums, the earliest gums in prehistory were not chicle based. Ancient peoples regularly chewed bark tar in the Mesolithic (9,000–4,000 BC) period in Scandinavia, Finland, Switzerland, and southern Germany. Ancient peoples like the Ertebølle, Maglemosian, and Konge-mose cultures would heat birch wood to a minimum of 800 degrees (based on the findings of replicative experiments) to force the tar to seep out. After collecting the tar, they would sometimes sweeten it with honey and chew on it. Although the birch bark tar also served to haft tools such as Ötzi the Ice Man's 5,300-year-old copper axe,[4] shapeless lumps with tooth impressions dating as far back as 9,000 years ago have been found in archaeological contexts in Bökeburg, Sweden. The size and shape of the tooth impressions indicate that the chewers were usually children and adolescents between the ages of six and fifteen. Besides simple chewing, the tar was probably also used for cleaning teeth and gums, or perhaps (extracting from the ethnographic record in Europe) to aid with congestion, toothaches, sore throats, stomach pains, heartburn, ringworm, and frostbite.[5]

The ancient Greeks chewed on a similar substance called "mastich," which is likely the root for the word *mastication*. In the ancient Greek encyclopedia *Natural History* from 77 BC, author Pliny the Elder describes mastich as coming from numerous plant sources with several levels of quality. The most desirable was a white mastich from the island of Chios in Greece, which was extracted from the lentisk or mastic tree (*Pistacia lentiscus*) and was mixed with resin. They also obtained gum from a prickly shrub found in India and Arabia, known as lama or laina, and an herb in Asia known as the terebinth (*Pistacia terebinthus*). The least desirable gum came from the cypress tree (*Cupressus sempervirenst)*, which was considered to be too acrid. In addition to being chewed, the gums had cosmetic and medicinal properties. The mastich produced from the lentisk was used as pomade for curling eyelashes and as a cream to smooth the skin and soothe abrasions. It was also believed to cure chronic coughs and the spitting of blood.[6]

The Great American Invention

Spruce Tree Gum

In North America, Native American Indians and Inuit have used gum from the spruce tree to waterproof canoes as well as for chewing. One Pima legend even describes a wind spirit telling a man and woman to collect the chewing gum to protect them from disaster. "Suha, you and your good wife are the only people worth saving. Go and make a large, hollow ball of spruce gum in which you and your wife can live as long as the coming flood will last." They obeyed the spirit, and after the great flood they emerged from their chewing gum ark to find that they were the only survivors on earth,[7] and the first bubble couple.

When European settlers came to New England, they adopted the indigenous custom of chewing on spruce tree resin. The hardened and sticky gum held up to chewing and had an unsweetened but woodsy taste. The gum ranged in color from amber to brown to pink, although collectors most preferred the amber color. Later, when lumberjacks began cutting down the forests, they supplemented their income by collecting and selling spruce resin to local merchants. The gum oozed naturally to protect the tree from injury and in its hardened form was relatively easy to collect from the felled tree and its stump. The two primary species used for spruce gum (as well as for timber and paper pulp) were black spruce (*Picea mariana* [Miller] Britton, Sterns & Pogg) and red spruce (*Picea rubens* Sarg).[8]

A New Englander by the name of John Curtis capitalized on the popularity of chewing resin and in 1848 invented the first commercial spruce tree gum. He and his son cleaned the resin by boiling it and removing any detritus, bugs, or bark, then poured it onto a slab and rolled it into sheets; they cut the sheets into strips, and to keep them from sticking together, bathed the strips in cornstarch. These were wrapped in tissue paper and sold in batches of twenty in a small wooden box. They named their invention "State of Maine Pure Spruce Gum" and began marketing it to local shopkeepers. It proved to be extremely popular, and within four years Curtis had built the world's first chewing gum factory in Portland,

Maine.[9] They sold their product nationwide, and soon after imitators began to sell their own brands of spruce gum. However, due to the tremendous amount of spruce-gum tapping and the increased demand for spruce wood pulp needed for making newspapers, the resin reserves were shrinking.[10] Another disadvantage to spruce gum was that although it was aromatic, the resin had a bitter aftertaste and became brittle after being chewed. By the 1920s there was only one producer of spruce gum left—Harry Davis, the self-proclaimed "Spruce Gum King," who catered to older customers who wanted to chew their childhood gum.[11] In the place of spruce gum, other small-scale producers prepared gums from ingredients such as beeswax, paraffin, and saps from the cherry and tamarack trees.[12]

The chewing gum that would come to dominate the world market was invented in the 1870s through an inadvertent connection between a New York family by the name of Adams and the exiled former president of Mexico, Antonio López de Santa Anna. The stories of how this association and invention came about vary *widely*.[13] As there are no written records that definitively document how they met, many of the tales are apocryphal. Some sources claim that a younger member of the Adams family (in one case a James Adams[14] and in other cases John Adams[15]) was hired as Santa Anna's secretary and came up with the idea after observing the general constantly chewing raw chicle. However, there is no evidence of this hire in Santa Anna's memoirs or other sources, and we do actually know that he had a personal secretary named Ralph Napegy. Still other sources maintain that Adams Sr. was Santa Anna's landlord or the owner of the boarding house in which he stayed and that one of the Adams boys found or stole the chicle in Santa Anna's dresser drawers.[16] Still another legend states that while Santa Anna was imprisoned in the United States after his capture at San Jacinto following the battle of the Alamo he was befriended by his jailor who asked him if he needed anything. Reportedly, he asked for the chicle latex of the sapodilla tree, as it had brought him great comfort as a child. The jailer was none other than one of the Adams sons—and chicle-based chewing gum was born.[17] How they really came to meet is a convoluted but intriguing history. My version of the story is based on an extensive review of the various sources and information taken directly from census data, obituaries, and family histories of the Adams family as well as biographies of López de Santa Anna.

The Adams Family and Antonio López de Santa Anna

Thomas Adams Sr. was born in New York City in 1818 and lived in the region until he died in 1905. During the Civil War he was appointed as a government photographer for three years, taking keepsake daguerreotype photos of members of the Union Army of the Potomac (Anon. 1934:17). He married Martha E. Dunbar (1824–?) and had seven children: three daughters, Carrie S. Case (1854–?), Grace E. Cave (1860–?), and Irene W. Adams (1862–?), and four sons, Thomas Jr. (1846–1926), John Dunbar (1849–1934), Horatio M. (1854–1956), and Garrison B. (1866–?).[18] After the war, he tried his hand as an inventor, creating a new kind of horse feed bag and a burner for kerosene lamps. Eventually he opened a successful store in Staten Island as a glass merchant.[19] Accounts indicate that he continued working on inventions in his spare time and that starting in 1866 his sons John, Thomas Jr., and Horatio assisted him in early experiments with using chicle as a new kind of rubber substitute.[20] All scholars seem to agree that the first chicle resin they used was obtained from the exiled Mexican president of Alamo fame, General Antonio López de Santa Anna.[21]

Antonio López de Santa Anna (1794–1876) was born in the city of Jalapa in the Mexican state of Veracruz to upper-class *criollo* (Mexicans of pure Spanish blood) parents. Against his parent's wishes, he went to a military academy instead of studying to become a businessman.[22] At the age of sixteen, he joined the Spanish army and fought against the liberation of Mexico from Spain. In 1821 he defected to the Mexican army he had previously fought against and was promoted to brigadier general by the time Mexico was freed from Spain that same year.[23] After his tenure as governor of Veracruz, he became president of Mexico in 1833, the first of his eleven terms.[24] In March of 1836, he temporarily resigned as president, marched into the Mexican province of Texas, and with over fifteen hundred men defeated the American defenders of the Alamo. Although the Mexicans won the battle, a large number of their soldiers had been killed or wounded during the fight, in part because Santa Anna did little to provide medical care for his men.[25] About one month later as Santa Anna and his men were camping at San Jacinto, Sam Houston led a surprise attack, killing four hundred Mexican soldiers, wounding two hundred, and taking seven hundred and thirty prisoners, including Santa Anna.[26] During his captivity, Santa Anna lobbied for his freedom by agreeing to command the Mexican troops to draw back from Texas and to remain south of the Rio Grande.[27] After signing the treaty that proclaimed Texas's independence in 1837, Santa Anna was released back to Mexico in disgrace.[28]

Despite having given up Texas, he regained his popularity in Mexico as a hero and martyr (he lost his left leg) during the "Pastry War" of 1838 between France and Mexico[29] and served as president for six more terms. During that time he moved in and out of Mexico for several years, living in Jamaica and Colombia, and eventually returning to Mexico in 1853 to serve his eleventh and final term as president. Mexico was in complete chaos by this time, having lost huge territories to the United States,[30] and was suffering from indigenous revolts and a treasury that was in shambles.[31] Realizing that he would soon be forced into exile, López de Santa Anna left in 1855 for Cuba, went back to Colombia, and then finally to the island of St. Thomas in the West Indies. While on St. Thomas he met U.S. Secretary of State William Seward, who was passing through on vacation. Word of their meeting spread, and eventually this news was used to swindle Santa Anna. An outcast Colombian revolutionary visited him, claiming he had just returned from Washington DC. He produced a forged letter supposedly from Seward that invited Santa Anna to New York to organize an expedition against the Napoleon III–backed leader Maximilian, then emperor of Mexico. Santa Anna was taken in by the ploy and bestowed forty thousand pesos to help fund the trip to the United States. Upon his arrival he leased an expensive house in New York City, entered into litigation with the ship owners who demanded further payment for his travel to the United States, and was soon broke. He eventually moved to a smaller house on Staten Island and hired Rudolph Napegy as his personal secretary and interpreter. Napegy befriended Thomas Adams Sr. around 1857 after spending time in his glass store and learning that he was an amateur inventor. Adams reported many years later: "when General Santa Anna was in this country, his secretary had with him a piece of this chicle. I saw the stuff and believed I could use it as a substitute for caoutchouc or India-rubber."[32] Adams and his son visited Santa Anna's Staten Island home and the general gave him a supply of chicle. Santa Anna had brought this with him from Mexico, in the hopes that he would be able to find someone who would be able to develop chicle as an alternative to rubber. If successful, it would have brought Adams and Santa Anna great riches and funded Santa Anna's return to power in Mexico. Adams Sr. and his sons began trying to replicate the vulcanization process discovered by Charles Goodyear in 1839, which included adding sulfur to allow the rubber to maintain its shape, increase its elasticity, and improve resistance to temperature changes.[33] However, after several unsuccessful attempts, Santa Anna lost interest.[34] Eventually, he returned to Mexico City, where he died in 1876, senile, impoverished, and unaware that the chicle latex he had left behind would change U.S. history.[35]

Adams paid to have additional chicle brought from Mexico and continued melting it down at different temperatures and with different additives, only to have it shred rather than bounce. He spent $30,000 of his own money trying to vulcanize it, without success.[36] According to his son Horatio, after a year of experimenting Thomas Sr. was ready to give up and throw the rest of the supply of chicle into the East River. Fortunately, while in a neighborhood drugstore he overheard a young girl ask for a piece of paraffin wax gum.[37] After speaking with the shopkeeper about the popularity of this waxy concoction, he remembered that the indigenous peoples of Mexico had chewed chicle as a kind of gum and was inspired to put the chicle to good use. When he got home, Thomas Sr. and his sons got to work and made the first chicle-based chewing gum in 1859. They boiled the chicle in a pot of hot water, and when it reached a puttylike consistency, they rolled it into small gray balls. They sold out their first batch at the local drugstore in hours and decided to go into the manufacturing business. With an investment of $55.00 they formed a new company named Adams and Sons in Jersey City and installed Thomas Sr. as the first company president.[38] They increased their production by steaming the chicle to remove any impurities and pouring it in a liquid state into molds rather than hand-rolling each piece.[39] They began selling their unflavored gum in local confectionary stores by providing free pieces with the purchase of candy.[40] When they later added sugar and flavoring, gum sales increased dramatically.[41]

In 1866, other U.S. manufacturers joined the gum manufacturing craze and began financing chicle tapping in Veracruz, Mexico.[42] By the late 1880s Adams gum was sold widely in the United States, and the company was employing over three hundred workers at the largest chewing gum plant in the world, located near the Brooklyn Bridge. They produced five tons of chewing gum daily. This included their best-selling Tutti Frutti gum, and Black Jack licorice gum, which was recommended for curing colds and is still sold today in limited quantities.[43] With the need for higher production, Thomas Adams Sr. made the first chewing gum machine in 1871.[44] The machine was placed in the local drugstores, where it kneaded a small supply of the sweetened chicle and pushed it into thin strips. A small-toothed blade notched the strips at regular intervals so that the salesperson could easily break it into sections and sell them for a penny.[45]

In 1888, Thomas Adams Sr. commissioned the first penny gum vending machine. When he had them placed in subway platforms, they became extremely popular and the family grew rich.[46] That same year, C.P.H. Gilbert, a twenty-five-year-old architect, designed a double-residence mansion with the first elevator in New York City for the Thomas Adams Jr. and John Dunbar Adams families. The rock-faced brownstone was located in Park Slope in Brooklyn across from the Feltman mansion, occupied by the inventor of the hotdog. Soon after moving in, the Adams families headed to their coastal home in Bay Shore, New York,[47] for the summer to avoid the heat. Six months later when they returned home, the servants did not answer their call. They entered the house, and when they rang for the elevator, it appeared to have gotten stuck. They soon learned that the four servants had become trapped in the elevator and had died of starvation and dehydration.[48] One local legend says that the servants survived for a time on Chiclets and that to this day residents can hear the sound of chewing in certain parts of the building.[49] It's a great urban legend but probably bogus. The Adams chewing gum company did not produce Chiclets until 1914, twenty-five years after the servants starved to death. Eventually the family sold the house; builders removed the elevator and turned the mansion into apartments.[50] Despite the elevator mishap, C.P.H. Gilbert went on to become one of the most sought-after residential architects on the Upper East Side of Manhattan.[51]

By 1919, the Adams family chewing gum manufacturing needs became so great that under the guise of the American Chicle Company, they spent $2 million building a massive five-and-a-half story, 550,000-square-foot concrete building in Long Island City. The building was noted for dedicating an entire half floor to employees, which included separate dining rooms for men and women, a large kitchen, lounges, recreation rooms, and restrooms.[52] It also included a central tower that was used to house the fire protection system and to improve

Figure 3.1. The Adams Gum/American Chicle Company factory in Long Island City, New York, around 1936. (Photograph courtesy of the Brooklyn Collection of the Brooklyn Public Library)

the appearance of the building (fig. 3.1).[53] The new building housed over five hundred employees and turned out five million packages of chewing gum a day, making Adams one of the most successful chewing gum companies in the world,[54] rivaled only by the iconic William Wrigley Jr. Company.

The Reign of William Wrigley Jr.

Another key figure in the burgeoning chewing gum industry was William Wrigley Jr. (1861–1932). The oldest of nine children and the son of a soap salesman, he was a highly spirited young man. At the age of eleven he ran away from his home in

Philadelphia to sell newspapers in New York City. He slept on the floor next to the newspaper presses of the *Tribune* building, or wrapped himself in newspapers and slept on the street. He also worked peeling potatoes in a boat galley and removing tar from boat rigging.[55] He came back to Philadelphia at the age of thirteen, only to be expelled from school for "having too much energy"—which he used to throw a cream pie on the nameplate of his eighth grade school. He worked for a year in his father's soap factory using a paddle to stir the soap ingredients in a large vat, but soon became restless and requested that he be allowed to work as a company traveling salesman. He argued that he looked older than his thirteen years, and, surprisingly, his father agreed to send him on the road to sell soap in Pennsylvania, New England, and New York. After four successful years, he grew weary of his sales circuit, and he planned to head west with a friend to mine gold and silver. On the way he lost their train tickets, and they were kicked off in Kansas City. He spent several years there and worked as a waiter, selling rubber stamps on the side. He eventually returned home to Philadelphia and worked as a soap salesman for another ten years.[56]

Wrigley moved to Chicago to open up a new branch of his father's soap company. At age thirty, he came up with the innovative idea to provide "premiums" to vendors with the purchase of certain amounts of soap. Although it meant that ultimately prices were slightly higher for the consumer, vendors got to keep items such as umbrellas, baking powder, and cookbooks, causing his sales to increase dramatically. Eventually he started giving away spruce and paraffin chewing gum with soap purchases; he quickly realized that the gum was more popular than the soap itself.[57] He decided to go into the chewing gum business and hired a paraffin wax producer by the name of Zeno Gum Company. He asked them to change the primary ingredient to chicle and produced several gum brands, including Vassar, Lotta, and Sweet Sixteen. He introduced Juicy Fruit and Wrigley's Spearmint in 1893, but needed to figure out a way to increase his sales to the vendors because the market was flooded with chewing gum brands. He offered premiums such as desks and cash registers to merchants who ordered a specific number of cases of gum; however, because gum was such a low-cost item, he often ended up losing money. He founded the fledgling William Wrigley Jr. Company in 1898 and decided that advertisements were the key to keeping his business afloat. He put ads for his gum in local newspapers, store windows, and on posters.[58] His business and savings slowly grew, and in 1902 he decided he wanted to move his company to New York City. Although he had saved $100,000 to put toward advertising, his advertisements and his product went almost completely unnoticed. Undaunted, he went to Chicago to save his money again so that he could increase his rate of advertising, a tactic that he promoted his whole life. As he told his son Philip many years later, "No matter what the condition of a business, never stop advertising."[59]

He returned to New York a second time, but this time to the more rural upstate area where his advertising money would go further and make a bigger impact. He advertised in every local newspaper, blanketed every streetcar he could find, and bought out all of the billboards in town. The marketing campaign was a great success, and by 1907 he had $250,000 to put toward advertising, overwhelming an economically depressed New York City with neon signs and large billboards. He dominated in advertising and garnered 60 percent of the chewing gum market. In 1915, he even sent a package of four sticks of spearmint chewing gum to all of the 1.5 million people listed in the U.S. phone book. In 1919 he created a chain of 117 billboards in the shape of gum wrappers that ran for a half mile along the Trenton-Atlantic City railway in New Jersey. It was a series of highly successful campaigns, and as a result, by the 1920s the William Wrigley Jr. Company employed twelve hundred people and turned out forty million sticks of gum a day.[60] His personal estate was valued at $150 million and included large mansions across the United States, ownership of most of Catalina Island off the southern coast of California, as well as controlling interest of the Chicago Cubs baseball team (fig. 3.2), who briefly trained on Catalina.[61] His wealth and power also meant that he was sometimes given unwanted attention, such as when the *New York Times* reported that he had experienced a breakdown due to overwork, or when he was (falsely) accused of being a member of the Ku Klux Klan.[62] Wrigley became an American business icon; he made the cover of *Time* magazine in October of 1929, and his image was even put on a ten-cent postage stamp in Belize (then British Honduras) for his role in supporting the chicle industry there.[63] When he died of heart disease in 1931 at the age of seventy,[64] he was one of the most influential and affluent men in the United States. He was not alone, however, in having made a fortune from selling chewing gum, as there were several "chewing gum kings."

Image redacted due to rights restrictions

Figure 3.2. William Wrigley Jr. throwing out the first ball at a Chicago Cubs baseball game. (Photograph courtesy of Transcendental Graphics/Getty Images)

The Cleveland Connection

Other dominant players in the chewing gum industry at the turn of the century included William J. White and Dr. E. E. Beeman, both of Cleveland, Ohio. White (1851–1923) was originally born in Allenwick, Canada, and migrated to the United States as a child. He held several odd jobs in his youth, and one source reported that while he was a cook for mule drivers in Kansas he met a chewing gum peddler who sold chicle-based gum rather than the usual spruce gum. White reputedly bought the recipe of the peddler's chewing gum and began experimenting with gum making.[65] However, it is more likely that he first became acquainted with chewing gum in Cleveland. After moving to Ohio, he met his wife while working for her father, the owner of a well-digging company. After the well-digging business closed down, he started working in a confectionary store and began experimenting with paraffin.[66] He eventually bought a paraffin gum manufacturing plant in 1876 and set to work on improving the product. The result was a paraffin gum known as "The Diamond," which he, his wife, and sons sold in the streets and to small stores.[67] He first came across chicle when the neighborhood grocer was mistakenly shipped a barrel of it and gave it to him. After experimenting with it in his kitchen, he found that mixing corn syrup with the chicle latex allowed for the addition of flavors. White invented "Yucatan," the first peppermint-flavored gum, which was cut into sticks and packaged in pink paper.[68]

By 1892, William J. White was the largest manufacturer of chewing gum in the United States, employing over three hundred people and turning out three to four tons a day. His estate grew to be valued at over $5 million, and he bought mansions, a horse farm and racetrack, and a yacht. He sailed his yacht to England to promote his gum abroad and reportedly had an audience with King Edward VII. He pressed his Yucatan gum on the astonished monarch and then used the experience to his advantage, running up sales by claiming the king had loved his product.[69] Although he was not well educated and lacked a political background, White even made a successful run as a Republican candidate for the U.S. Congress in 1892. Rumor insisted that he secured his win in part by distributing chewing gum to local voters.[70] He was also well known as a womanizer, who was frequently seen with beautiful young women, including stage and silent-movie star Anna Held. Although he and his wife had lived apart for six years, she was reluctant to agree to a divorce. In 1906, a very public court case dissolved the marriage and White remained in New York.[71]

The more subdued Dr. E. E. Beeman (1840–1906) was a pharmacist who manufactured pepsin, a by-product of pigs' intestines, which he discovered helped with indigestion. He sold the product in glass bottles with a pig on the label, but sales were slow. One day when he was visiting a local stationery store, a young female clerk suggested that he should add pepsin to chewing gum and promote it for chewing after meals as a cure for heartburn. He invented pepsin gum, keeping the pig logo on the original packaging. Eventually, an investor in his company suggested that this emblem was inappropriate, saying, "You are not selling sausage, but a delectable confection." Eventually, Beeman agreed to use his own image and his picture on billboards, in newspapers, and on the gum label. He became known as the "Chewing Gum King" after making millions off of his investment, and said that he always took good care of the young woman who had originally suggested the invention by providing her with stock in the company.[72] In the meantime, other small business owners were busy concocting their own future icons of the chewing gum world.

The Fleer Brothers

Robert Fleer (1865–1937) and his brother Frank, owners of the Fleer Chewing Gum Company in Philadelphia were the inventors of the world-famous "Chiclets" gum.[73] This was the first candy-coated gum, which was apparently inspired by the coating commonly used on Jordan almonds at that time.[74] The Fleer brothers eventually sold their invention to American Chicle in 1914, which became one of the company's greatest acquisitions and biggest sellers. The candy coating kept the gum fresher for longer and facilitated exporting to the United Kingdom, the Philippines, Japan, China, and France.[75] American Chicle told the Fleer brothers that they were allowed to continue in the gum business only if they came up with products unrelated to Chiclets. Fortunately for them, one of their employees did this. In 1928, Walter Diemer, an accountant with the company, began experimenting with various types of gum base and unwittingly created bubble gum. He used a rubbery tree latex whose source he would not reveal, but said it was less sticky and more elastic than chicle. The bubble gum was colored pink because it was the only food coloring shade Diemer had on hand. After selling out of a batch of the gum in an afternoon, he presented his invention to the Fleer brothers, who adopted the recipe and called it "Dubble Bubble." They sold it in bright yellow wrappers similar to those used for taffy and taught their salesmen to blow bubbles as part of their sales pitch. Despite the popularity of their penny-a-piece product, they had little direct competition until Topps Chewing Gum, Inc. began making Bazooka bubble gum after World War II.[76]

The Beech-Nut Packing Company

Another key gum manufacturer was Bartlett Arkell (1862–1946), who was born in Canajoharie, New York, to a prominent family. His father, W. J. Arkell, had been a New York state senator and founded the Judge Publishing Company, which published *Demarest Magazine*, *Leslie's Weekly*, and *Judge*.[77] Arkell was a magazine editor for his father's company for ten years, as well as a paper bag manufacturer, a rug importer, and in 1891 the head of the Imperial Packing Company that he founded with a family friend in Canajoharie. His company, which he reigned over as president for fifty years, focused on the packaging and distribution of ham, bacon, and lard. The business languished until the turn of the century when he sold his paper bag factory and reinvested the money in the newly renamed Beech-Nut Packing Company. He was also a pioneer in the food packing business using glass containers and vacuum packing for food. As the company grew, they expanded their offerings with peanut butter, coffee, dried beef, chopped foods, soups—and, in 1911, Beech-Nut chewing gum.[78] The gum, which was a high-end line that contained a higher ratio of chicle and was chewier than most gums, became one of the best-selling brands in the United States.[79] With his success, Arkell became known as a patron of the arts and a generous employer for providing health insurance, pensions, and Christmas bonuses.[80]

In the 1930s and 1940s Arkell developed several promotions to publicize his company's products. These included the hiring of young women known as the "Beech-Nut gum girls" to distribute candy and gum, as well as a traveling circus. In 1931, Arkell and Beech-Nut Packing Company even contracted Amelia Earhart to fly one of their two Pitcairn autogyro planes from Newark, New Jersey, to Oakland, California, and back (fig. 3.3). With the publicity generated from this weeklong flight, as well as financial assistance from Beech-Nut, Earhart was able to embark upon several of her better-known flights, including New York to Europe in 1932, Hawaii to Oakland in 1935, and her ill-fated 1937 flight around the world.[81] Between the attention that Beech-Nut received from his various marketing schemes and his success at selling a wide range of products, Arkell was able to maintain a healthy and independent company throughout his tenure.

Image redacted due to rights restrictions

Figure 3.3. Amelia Earhart climbing into the Beech-Nut plane that she flew for her trans-Atlantic flight. (Photograph courtesy of New York Times Company/Getty Images)

The Chewing Gum Trust—American Chicle Company

Other companies saw advantage in combining forces, and in 1899 William J. White (W. J. White and Son), E. E. Beeman (Beeman Chemical Company), and Thomas Adams Jr. (Adams and Sons) merged with several other smaller production plants, including J. P. Primly (Chicago, Illinois), Kisme Gum (Louisville, Kentucky), and S. T. Briton (Toronto, Canada).[82] It was known informally as the "Chewing Gum Trust" and formally as "American Chicle Company." Thomas Adams Jr. was instituted as the first chairman.[83] Two years later, the company issued additional stock to secure capital to invest in chicle extraction and manufacturing in the Yucatán Peninsula.[84] Over several years, the trust gradually acquired the Sen-Sen Chiclet Company, Sterling Gum Company, and the Dentyne Company, turning out several popular gum brands, including Adams gum, Black Jack, Beeman's Pepsin gum, Sen-Sen Breathlets, Dentyne, and Chiclets.[85]

William J. White had a falling-out with the American Chicle Company, as others on the board of directors disliked his womanizing, flashy lifestyle, and the lavish budget he spent for advertising his own gum, and voted him out in 1905.[86] However, one source reports that White had his revenge. Reputedly, after his removal, the remaining gum manufacturers in the trust wanted to drive him out of business forever by cornering the market supply of raw chicle and driving up the price. The trust allegedly sent men down to the coast of Mexico to build up their supply of latex; however, Mr. White, hearing about the scheme, sent his own men down and had them seek out chicle sources inland. After collecting a large supply at a price of about twenty-five cents a pound, he had the chicle shipped north in secret. In the meantime, the scheme backfired on the trust when the price of chicle went to $1.25 and White wouldn't buy any of it, causing them to lose hundreds of thousands of dollars.[87] This plan also highlighted the general attitude of U.S. gum corporations toward the Latin American chicle companies; they wanted to pay the lowest market price for the highest yield of chicle, with little concern for the sustainability or viability of the raw product or the workers who collected it.[88]

¿Viva el Chicle? U.S. Corporations and Latin America

Turmoil in Latin American Chicle Extraction

While a few major manufacturers in the United States were making millions on chewing gum, they were also having a major impact on the chicle extraction industry of Latin America. The majority of chicle was coming out of Mexico and was controlled primarily by the William Wrigley Jr. Company, Beech-Nut Packing Company, and American Chicle Company. Although Guatemala also commanded large chicle resources, its remoteness and transportation costs made

Mexico a cheaper, more reliable source for foreign producers. Belize (British Honduras) had similar access to a high-quality product, but to increase yields chicle collectors often mixed it with inferior grades and varieties, making it less desirable to North American corporations that were concerned with quality control. The raw product was purchased directly from brokers and native producers and was often the sole source of income in some Maya towns.[89] Workers in Mexico, Guatemala, and Belize became highly dependent on North American corporations buying their product, and fluctuations in the prices and rate of purchases had a huge impact on their countries' economies. This unsustainable industry set into motion another so-called collapse of Maya civilization that continues to have an effect today.

The tumultuous relationship with the U.S. manufacturers started early on, beginning with bad weather that struck southern Mexico and Central America in 1904, resulting in a chicle shortage. This led to a dramatic spike in prices on top of the 10 cent per pound duty already being paid to the U.S. government, and caused the corporations to rethink the importation process. Within that same year, roughly 90 percent of the raw material used by U.S. gum companies was imported into Canada, processed, and then imported into the United States so that duty costs would be reduced.[90] As a result of the increase in cost, Wrigley's and Beech-Nut attempted to procure large stands of virgin forest in the Yucatán Peninsula, Belize, and Guatemala. In the Mexican state of Campeche, North American companies, including the Laguna Corporation, Pennsylvania Campeche Land and Lumber, and Mexican Gulf and Lumber were controlling roughly 800,000 hectares of forest.[91]

The Mexican government had only recently regained control of Quintana Roo, which had the largest stands of sapodilla trees, after nearly a half century of Maya resistance. During this Caste War (1847–1901), Maya dissidents had successfully retained power over much of the interior of the peninsula, in part because they provided timber to the Belizean government in exchange for supplies and weapons. Mexico (under the leadership of Mexican president Porfirio Díaz) and Belize (ruled by Queen Victoria) approved the Mariscal-Spencer Treaty in 1889, which prohibited the trade of ammunition and firearms to the Maya and defined the border between the two countries. By the turn of the century, Porfirio Díaz was encouraging foreign investment[92] and wanted to squelch the perception of Maya rebels as an obstacle to development. In 1902, the government formed the territory of Quintana Roo, and put the military in place to help control the Maya living in the region.[93] The local population was extremely small, numbering only 9,100 people according to the 1910 Mexican census.[94] Nonetheless, the Maya continued to maintain control of the central part of the territory, and their leaders negotiated the price of any chicle purchased from the area.[95] As a result, the extraction of chicle was generally concentrated in the northern and southern portions of Quintana Roo.[96] However, in 1915, the Mexican Revolution interrupted the production of chicle in Mexico and subsequently Guatemala, as it caused many of the chicleros and loggers in the bordering Petén region to move out of the area. Guatemalan chicle production was further reduced in 1916, when forces working against the tyrannical Guatemalan president Manuel Estrada Cabrera demolished the successful logging and chicle company known as Arthes and Sons.[97] The shortages caused U.S. corporations to begin seeking out new sources of chicle in Panamá, Honduras, Venezuela, and Colombia. For a few years these countries exported thousands of pounds of raw chicle. However, this plan was soon thwarted by the inferior quality of the latex as compared to Mexican and Central American chicle, high production and transportation costs, and labor conflicts.[98]

In 1918, under the orders of President Venustiano Carranza, the Mexican government defined ten large concessions within the borders of the new territory of Quintana Roo. They gave foreign companies seven land grants and reserved only three for national companies.[99] In Guatemala by the early 1920s, agents from American Chicle and Wrigley's had garnered control of the two largest concessions in Petén.[100] The chicle extraction industry developed rapidly and soon became one of the largest exports of Mexico[101] and Guatemala. In the territory of Quintana Roo alone, chicle production grew from 45,291 kilos in 1917 to 325,123 kilos in 1918. Within four years, the workers were extracting just under a million kilos.[102]

To support this demand, infrastructure for removal of the latex from the forest had to grow along with it. Companies modeled the labor organization after that used in lumber extraction in industrialized countries and imposed a hierarchical management structure. They created administrative centers, transport systems, and work camps much like those built for the lumber industry.[103] In Quintana Roo, infrastructure included inland production centers and hacienda houses for the managers, with narrow-gauge railroad lines that ran from the production houses to the coast, and a series of temporary camps placed strategically along the line near water sources.[104] U.S. companies enticed laborers with the promise of cash advances (sometimes paying more to those with experience), as well as providing clothing, food, and all supplies needed for tapping chicle in company stores.[105] In Guatemala, companies gave *contratistas* (jobbers) credit to purchase large equipment, and they in turn would give cash advances to the chicleros to equip themselves. The jobber would also provide the workers' families with monthly payments as well as supply the chicleros with medicine, food, and supplies during the working season. Chicleros had to sign a contract agreeing to provide a set amount of chicle latex for the season, from which the monthly payments and expenses would be deducted. Although some experienced workers profited under this system, others were exploited by paying high costs for supplies and taxes and suffered financial ruin.[106]

There was generally a large turnover in the labor force, but work was always available in the chicle industry during this period. The need for high production levels of good quality chicle was compounded by a dramatic increase in gum chewing at the start of World War I. William Wrigley Jr., in typical fashion, initiated mass media advertising techniques to convince the public that gum chewing was an excellent way to reduce tension. He pushed the idea that "the 'American habit' was a relief for nervous tension,[107] an aid to digestion, and, in the absence of water fit to drink, a mitigation of thirst."[108] As a result, the American military provided gum in soldiers' kit bags to help keep them alert and divert their attention away from thirst and hunger when in battle. Soldiers then spread the gum-chewing habit through Europe and particularly in the United Kingdom and Italy. Exports to Europe prior to World War I were at approximately $200,000 annually and jumped ten times that to nearly $2,000,000 per year after the war.[109] Meanwhile, the gum obsession was rampant back home. By the mid-1920s, the United States had become the largest consumer of gum, chewing 75 percent of the gum produced.[110] U.S. companies were importing 84,647,000 pounds of raw chicle annually, to help supply the average person with 105 sticks of gum per year.[111]

The booming 1920s forced to the forefront problems that plagued the chicle extraction industry in Mexico and Central America. The Cruzob, or rebel Maya, who had been rebelling against the mestizos (people of mixed European and indigenous blood) and Mexican government since the time of the Caste War, had maintained a military structure and had funded their supply of ammunition and arms by trading hardwoods with the British. They learned that chicle paid even more than wood and began smuggling it into Belize. Eventually, they became involved in the actual control of the resource through more official channels.[112] In an attempt to protect the lucrative chicle industry from within, the Mexican government appointed the Cruzob Maya leader Francisco May as a military commander of the territory of Quintana Roo. May was the stepson of a local rebel Maya chief, Felipe Yama, and had learned from his stepfather to be an aggressive leader. General May worked his newfound power to his advantage and became a liaison for the gum manufacturers, in particular Wrigley's, La Compañia Mexicana from Mexico, and a Cuban contractor named Julio Martín. May saw the money earned from chicle as a way to continue to fund the rebellion, and he provided armed protection for the surrounding chicle camps and controlled all local trade.[113] May was even transported to Mexico City to meet with President Portes Gil, where he assured him that he would do everything he could to keep peace in the region.[114] Portes Gil commissioned him as a general in the Mexican army and even provided him with a fancy uniform and ceremonial sword. With his newfound influence, he was able to garner the support of Felipe Carrillo Puerto, then governor of Yucatán, to have new schools built in Quintana Roo. May also received control of the railroad from Santa Cruz to Vigía Chico and twenty thousand hectares of land. Unfortunately, May abused this power and led a strict regime, effectively controlling the local population through physical punishment. May had disciplined a local chiclero with fifty lashes for not showing up to work in the jungle, who then reported the injustice to a local paper. Eventually word spread back to Mexico City and May's power was revoked in 1929 and transferred to the Mexican state.[115]

At this time, tensions also began to increase between Guatemala and Belize over the exportation of chicle. Prior to the 1930s, most of the chicle produced in the Petén region was smuggled to Belize to avoid Guatemalan exportation taxes. "Guatemalans were infuriated at the export of chicle from Belize, since they assumed that most if not all of this total represented the fruits of smuggling."[116]

Belizean pirates were also raiding the coast of Quintana Roo and taking chicle from camps that were preparing to send the cargo to the United States.[117] The Mexican government reported that the pirates were getting their information about when and where to raid from the chicleros, who were in a war with their employers. This employee-employer tension came to a head in August of 1929, when the Maya laborers staged a revolt against the chicle industry in Quintana Roo over inhumane working conditions. Several people, including workers and management, were wounded or killed. The North American corporations seemed to show little concern about the mutiny, as they viewed the chicleros as an isolated population and did not expect the revolt to spread to other areas. Additionally, the general attitude of U.S. citizens at the time was that the workers were primitive and backward, as reflected in this statement from the *New York Times*: "Only a few of the Maya Indians understand Spanish and practically all of them are heathens worshipping a three-headed god, using the Catholic ritual and Spanish and Latin words which were taught to their ancestors by sixteenth century missionaries. . . . The modern Mayas have degenerated far from their cultured ancestors."[118] To squelch the rebellion, the Mexican secretary of war dispatched the Thirty-Sixth federal battalion of 350 men from Veracruz to Cozumel and then sent smaller detachments to guard chicle collection centers such as Santa María and Santa Cruz. By 1930, buyers of chicle began to offer far less for cured chicle, and the collectors were irate. They blamed General May for the crash and responded by stopping their collecting temporarily.[119] North American collectors responded by buying their latex from regions outside of the rebel Maya areas.

During the early 1930s, Mexico contributed 77 percent, or fourteen million pounds, of the chicle used by U.S. manufacturers, while Guatemala exported around 22 percent, with the remaining 1 percent coming primarily from Belize. By the mid-1930s, however, serious concerns were arising about the sustainability of extraction, as careless tapping was estimated to have killed 25 percent of the sapodilla trees in Mexico. In 1942 nearly four million kilos of chicle was extracted just from the Yucatán Peninsula and sold to Beech-Nut, Wrigley's, American Chicle Company, and Clark Brothers.[120] Although the Tropical Plant Research Foundation had undertaken a major study in Mexico, Guatemala, and Belize in the mid-1930s to attempt to improve tapping methods of the sapodilla tree,[121] overtapping was occurring. This was compounded by the fact that chicleros were paid by the pound, and they were inclined to obtain the greatest harvest in the shortest amount of time. This meant that they often disregarded sustainable methods for harvesting the crop and tapped trees when they were too young, or retapped before proper healing had occurred (generally less than three to eight years). This made the trees susceptible to attack by insects, bacteria, and fungus, often resulting in death.[122] Researchers working for the Chicle Research Project under the auspices of the Tropical Plant Research Foundation conducted small-scale studies in Belize, Guatemala, and Mexico to try to find new sources of latex to replace the sapodilla tree, but yields of other species were consistently lower.[123] They also sought to find out whether sapodilla trees would respond like rubber trees by increasing their yield if they were tapped daily. The unhappy findings were that sapodilla trees were unresponsive and could not be tapped to the same level of rubber trees.[124] These factors combined with the high demand for raw chicle sparked the speculation that the intensive scale of extraction in Latin America could not be maintained for more than another twenty-five to forty years without totally depleting the forests.[125]

By the early 1940s, under the guidance of President Lázaro Cárdenas, the Mexican state controlled and suppressed the Maya rebels and began regulating the manufacture of chicle through the use of cooperatives. Most sapodilla trees were located on *ejido* (communally owned) or federal land, making them common property. Previously chicleros had access to these regions based on tradition and personal influence, but were now under government regulation through the cooperative system.[126] The cooperatives, which included approximately twenty thousand workers, were run under the auspices of the Agricultural Ministry and the Banco de Comercio Exterior. In 1943, representatives from the Mexican chicle cooperatives traveled to the United States to "discuss and defend the price of chicle, one of the most appreciated wartime materials in the United States." During their meetings they emphasized that the Mexican government had added small airstrips in the Yucatán Peninsula that shortened the time needed for transport of shipments to the coast, where they could then be loaded onto boats and transported to the United States.[127] However, their attempt to control the price of chicle ultimately hurt them.

Some North American companies, out of fear of chicle shortages and increased prices, purchased large areas of land in Latin America and propagated chicle plantations. This was despite the fact that the yields would take years because of the need for trees to reach bearing age.[128] Gum manufacturers also sought out new regions outside of Latin America for raw materials to use in gums, such as jelutong and gutta siak latexes from British Malaya and the East Indies and wild fig latex from Africa.[129] This greatly worried the chicle-collecting industries in Mexico, Guatemala, and Belize, as this had been one of their largest industries.[130] Additional threats to the Latin American chicle harvesting industry came about in the mid-1940s with an increase in U.S. import and export taxes, and with the development of petroleum-based synthetics as a substitute for chewing gum base.[131] Although the exact recipes of synthetic gum bases are generally kept as trade secrets, they commonly include a mixture of natural latexes such as jelutong or chicle, paraffin wax or beeswax, and polyethylene, polyvinyl acetate, and stearic acid. The need for large amounts of low-cost gum base was further inflated during the Korean War (1950–53) after the U.S. military continued to include chewing gum in the rations of soldiers.[132]

Strife within U.S. Chewing Gum Companies

In addition to the issues with the Latin American extraction industry, there were battles being waged within and between U.S. chewing gum manufacturers between the 1920s and 1950s. To start with, all was not well within the walls of the ever-growing American Chicle Company. The company stockholders formed the Stockholders Protective Committee in 1924 to remove the corporate control of the Bank Creditors Committee that had been in place since 1922. The committee, which included John F. Adams, claimed that mismanagement, and not competition, had resulted in gum sales falling from $14 million to $4 million since the takeover. They also revealed that the company had been offered to their main competitor in 1923 without knowledge of the stockholders or the board of directors.[133]

Smaller gum-manufacturing companies had begun to close across the United States. They were unable to match the amounts the major companies were spending on advertising, and they lacked the brand-name loyalty of the more established companies. The expense of machinery was also prohibitive, and they had difficulty in obtaining enough raw materials at a low enough price.[134] Larger companies had the advantage of being able to buy in bulk and had manufacturing plants strategically located near seaports that provided much easier access to imported ingredients.[135] By 1935, the three main North American manufacturers produced 95 percent of gum consumed in the United States. The William Wrigley Jr. Company dominated the market by producing roughly 60 percent, while the Beech-Nut Packing Company produced 20 percent and the American Chicle Company 15 percent.[136] One smaller plant, known as Topps Chewing Gum, Inc. and run by the Shorin brothers in Brooklyn, managed to break into the market by selling themselves as a "change maker." The brothers instructed cashiers to encourage customers to buy penny pieces of Topps chewing gum, instead of receiving a few pennies in change.[137]

World War II also had an impact on gum manufacturing and sales. Although sales of chewing gum in 1941 exceeded $20 million, by 1942 there was a 10–15 percent decline due to rationing in sugar supplies. Even though the corporations kept up to a year's worth of supplies in stock, the government was restricting sugar use from the previous year by 20 percent.[138] Despite the supply shortages and a scarcity of skilled labor in the United States, chewing gum companies announced that temporarily closing the chicle companies would do little good toward the war effort since the majority of their employees were young women and the job of wrapping sticks of gum was considered unskilled.[139] Overall, the domestic consumption of gum was strained because of the more than 600 million sticks of gum that soldiers chewed every year, leaving little for the civilian population. In 1944, the Wrigley Company announced that their manufacturing would be restricted to only providing gum for the U.S. Army and Navy and that civilians would be limited to the current stocks already in storage.[140] Because of chicle shortages, Philip Wrigley, president and son of the founder, sent researchers around the world to seek out new ingredients that could be used for gum base and limited his company's production to "wartime chewing gum," discontinuing the manufacturing of its standard brands until enough raw ingredients could be obtained.[141] Despite these shortages, the chewing gum habit took hold and dominated popular culture in the Americas.

Chewing Gum and Popular Culture: Bazooka Joe, Baseball Cards, and Bad Manners

After World War II, civilian chewing gum production increased and new brands were introduced. One of the most popular was the Topps Chewing Gum company's Bazooka Joe, which was first launched in 1947. In 1953, a comic strip was added to the gum in the hopes of drawing more interest. Bazooka Joe was created by two artists who had previously worked on the early animated Popeye and Superman cartoons. Joe dressed like a typical 1950s teenager with rolled-up jeans and a white T-shirt, but was made unique by wearing a mysterious eye patch. Over the decades several friends were added to the strip, and the main characters such as Mort and Hungry Herman became American icons.[142] Bazooka Joe's popularity spread, and, starting in 1957, Topps permitted an Argentine company to make and sell Bazooka gum in Argentina, Bolivia, Chile, Paraguay, and Uruguay.[143] After the strip and its characters had gone through several transformations over the decades, in 2006 Bazooka Joe went through a $4 million makeover in an attempt to make him more contemporary. In addition to now having ripped jeans and wild hair, Joe made some new friends, including Wolfgang Spreckets, a German exchange student who played the electric guitar, and Cindy Lewis, an environmentalist who loved hiking and recycling. The company hoped that the gum and comic strip would continue to appeal to today's youth, as well as to adults who chewed it when they were young.[144]

Chewing gum also continued to grow in popularity through its association with collectible cards. Card collecting started in the 1870s when cigarette manufacturers included pictures of Civil War generals, flags, and ships, and then in 1886, baseball cards. During the 1930s, Bowman Gum issued the first chewing gum cards, which included a war series.[145] During World War II the Topps Chewing Gum corporation released a number of card series, including plane spotter cards (to teach civilians how to identify enemy planes), the "Freedoms Wars," world leaders and events, and flags of the United Nations.[146] In 1952, an employee by the name of Sy Berger decided to issue baseball cards for Topps. For five cents a purchaser received chewing gum and a pack of six free cards with a color picture on the front and statistics on the back.[147]

In the early 1960s Topps expanded their cards to include images of stars such as the Beatles, Elvis Presley, television idols William Boyd as Hopalong Cassidy and Fess Parker as Davy Crockett, as well as politicians such as Lyndon B. Johnson.[148] In 1962, the Federal Trade Commission charged that Topps had a monopoly on baseball cards, although three years later they ruled that their nearly exclusive control of photographs of baseball players was not the equivalent of an illegal hold on the market.[149] Topps continued to sell the collectible cards with chewing gum until 1991, when they caved to the pressure of collectors who said that the gum stained the cards. In 2001 they reintroduced gum into their fiftieth anniversary card series, with the chewing gum wrapped in cellophane.[150] Although they have sold millions of cards over the last fifty plus years, Sy Berger said, "All we wanted to do was sell bubble gum. . . . We really had no idea if the cards would sell. We were neophytes. There was no way anyone could have imagined that it would turn out like this."[151] Topps has continually outsold their competitors, even though the Fleer Chewing Gum Company challenged Topps in the court and in the marketplace. Starting in 1975, Fleer accused Topps of maintaining a monopoly through exclusive contracts with baseball players for their images, but the decisions of the suits were continually overturned in Topps's favor.[152] The Fleer Company eventually found a loophole. As Topps's contracts with baseball players stated, Topps had exclusive rights over all baseball *cards* packaged alone or with candy such as gum. Fleer began selling cards without gum, but with stickers of major league logos instead.[153]

Chewing gum even became a part of popular songs in the United States, such as Grand Ole Opry star Uncle Dave Macon's 1930s signature song "Two in One—Chewing Gum" and the 1950s Lonnie Donegan hit, "Does Your Chewing Gum Lose Its Flavor on the Bedpost Overnight?" In Latin America, numerous songs have incorporated the topic of chicle. Former chiclero Policarpo Aguilar, who worked in Mexico and Belize, became a musician as an older man and sang romantic songs such as "Chiclero" about the jungle and his culture. The Mexican band Chalo Campos y Su Orquesta released a greatest hits album in 2006 with the song "El Chiclero," and Juan Fernando Montaño recorded a Merengue dance hit entitled "El Chiclet."[154] In Mexico, the term "chicle" has become regularly incorporated into slang phrases such as "Ya deja a tus amigos en paz, no seas chicle" (Don't stick so close to your friends; don't be annoying); "Ya llegaste con tu chicle pegado" (You arrived with someone who is unwelcome); and "Lo trataste como a tu chicle masticado" (You chewed [him/her] up and spit [him/her] out).[155] In mid-twentieth-century movies in the United States, gum was regularly used as a prop to identify lowly characters such as carhops, gangsters, and prostitutes, while the lead characters were never seen chewing it.[156] In Mexico and much of Latin America, gum is placed in piñatas and is a staple at most holidays and celebrations. A plethora of novelty gums are available, and images of pop culture and sports are regularly reflected in the packaging.[157]

Emily Post, the authority on good manners, refused to even mention gum chewing in her book *Etiquette* (first published in 1922) until the 1950s, and even then it was only to emphasize that it was a poor habit. "It is still impossible to imagine a lady walking on a city street and either chewing gum or smoking."[158] By the 1960s she had eliminated any discussion of gum chewing etiquette once again,[159] but in her most current volumes she offers a few pieces of advice: "Cracking gum, smacking it, or chomping away in a mechanical rhythm can be disturbing or distracting to many people, especially in close quarters. In public, chew gum discretely and dispose of it in a waste receptacle—never on the ground. . . . Young people must understand that watching someone chew gum is, as older generations say, 'like watching a cow chew its cud.'"[160] Although polite society has respected this advice, many have been horrified with the enthusiastic embrace of the "American habit" around the world. Despite the tremendous popularity that gum has enjoyed, many view the chewing habit negatively and as a poor reflection of U.S. culture. In 1898 a British newspaper reported that health officials were issuing warnings against "American chewing gum," which was considered even more dangerous than Italian ice cream.[161]

Leon Trotsky, the Bolshevik revolutionary, once commented: "Thus it is with these people in the subway. . . . Capital does not like the working man to think and is afraid. . . . It has therefore adopted measures. . . . It has put up automats in each station and has filled them with disgusting candied gum. With an automatic movement of the hand the people extract from these automats pieces of sweetish gum, and they grind it with the automatic chewing of their jaws. . . . It looks like a religious rite, like some silent prayer to God-Capital."[162] This negative view is still prevalent, as was recently demonstrated when the Argentinean singer Piero released the socially critical song "Los Americanos":

Si conocen historia	If they know history
no es por haber leído	it is not from having read it
sino por haberla visto	but by having seen it
en el cine americano.	in American movies.
Con grandes escenarios	With grand stages
y música grandiosa	and magnificent music
en sutíl estilo	in the subtle style
de los americanos.	of the Americans.
De mandíbulas grandes	With big mouths
de tanto mascar chiclets	from having chewed gum so much
es muy común el verlos	it is common to see
a los americanos.[163]	the Americans.

The Bubble Bursts: The Downfall of the Chicle Industry

Ultimately, the incredible popularity of chicle-based chewing gum in the mid-twentieth century led to its own downfall. The problems of overtapping the sapodilla trees to meet this demand and the development of lower-cost petroleum-based polymer gum substitutes resulted in the decline of chicle exportation.[164] Additionally, Guatemala and Mexico, in a valorous attempt to protect their natural resources, ultimately hurt their exportation business. As they improved regulations on exploiting forest resources and increased export taxes on chicle, the long-term result was a lower demand by foreign companies.[165] In 1952, the Wrigley Company announced that they would no longer purchase chicle in Guatemala due to high prices (resulting from export taxes) and the lower cost of the use of synthetics. This was predicted to be a loss of $2 million annually to the Guatemalan government.[166] Exportation continued to decrease in Latin America during the 1950s and 1960s. Most of the railroads in Quintana Roo were abandoned and sold for scrap by the 1970s, and the Mexican workforce declined to only 4,800 by the end of the decade.[167] As of 1976, Japan's Mitsui Company surpassed the United States in its exportation of chicle from Petén, and continues to this day to be the largest importer of Guatemalan latex.[168] In 1980, the United States terminated the importation of chicle from Mexico entirely, as the supply of natural latex had simply become too unreliable and the petroleum-based substitutes could be obtained easily and at such a low cost.[169]

By the 1970s, gum manufacturing had changed dramatically, and the processing of synthetic gums was done in huge spotless, air-conditioned factories. The manufacturing plants were filled with workers in white uniforms, who produced the chewing gum without ever touching it. A machine would grind up the gum base, made up primarily of natural and synthetic gum bases, into small pieces, and place it on trays in a hot room to be dried out for two days. Workers then placed the ingredients into a huge kettle and melted them at 240°F until they turned into heavy syrup. They strained the syrup through a fine mesh for any impurities, clarified it in a centrifuge, and sent it to the industrial vats with giant mixing blades. Workers introduced additional ingredients based on a formula for each brand of gum, which ensured consistency in the flavor and texture. Powdered sugar, corn syrup, and softeners, such as vegetable oils, were included to sweeten, moisten, and make the mixture chewable. Once the gum had the texture of bread dough, they added the natural or artificial flavorings. When it had been mixed enough times and was at the correct temperature, the mixer squeezed big globules onto cooling belts. The gum ran along a conveyer belt through a cooling tunnel filled with air currents and then was sent to a kneader for a few hours to make it smooth. The mixture was then cut into smaller loaf-shaped sections to make it easier to work with.

From this point, the process differed depending on the type of gum being produced. One machine squeezed the gum out into thin ribbons like a tube of toothpaste and cut it into gum balls, which were covered with a candy coating and beeswax to make them shine. Other types of gum were sent through roller machines that flattened the loaf-shaped chunks into sheets. Like the original spruce gum producers who used cornstarch, the machines bathed the sheets in powdered sugar to keep them from sticking. The machine then removed the thicker sheets to cut them into small pieces of candy-coated or bubble gum, and thinner sheets were made into stick gum. The sheets were cut into single sticks but were kept together on stacks of trays and placed in a temperature- and humidity-controlled room for a minimum of two days for a process known as "conditioning." This curing process kept the gum fresher for a longer period of time. The final step was to package the gum. Machines broke the sheets up into separate sticks, applied paper and aluminum wrappers, and sealed them, making them ready to be shipped.[170]

U.S. companies have continued to experiment with synthetic chewing gums, and several innovations have been made, including sugar-free gums like Trident and gums that can be chewed by denture wearers. In 1975, Wrigley's introduced Freedent, the first nonstick gum.[171] Apparently, the company had been attempting to deal with this issue since 1960, when Philip K. Wrigley announced they were patenting dentures to which gum would not stick.[172] Additionally, in the late 1960s, nicotine chewing gum was developed in Sweden with the idea that smokers could help kick their habit by taking in a less harmful form of nicotine. In the early 1970s it was tested for safety and effectiveness in Canada, England, and Sweden.[173] What became "Nicorette" gum was approved in 1984 by the Food and Drug Administration and made available to smokers by prescription.[174] Although there was concern that smokers could become addicted to the gum or that it came with its own health risks, investigators determined that the gum might ultimately help smokers quit.[175]

Other gum technologies have been introduced recently, including a gum developed in 1998 by sleep researcher Gary Kamimori that could deliver caffeine to the body. The U.S. Congress provided funding a year later to develop and study the effects of the gum. Kamimori's conclusions were that the act of chewing delivered the caffeine to the human system four to five times more quickly than a liquid or pill because it is absorbed into the tissues of the mouth. The U.S. Army became interested in the potential for the product and in 2006 announced that it was supplying "Stay Alert" caffeine gum to their troops in military operations to help with problems of fatigue. Each piece of chewing gum contains 100 mg of caffeine, which is roughly the equivalent of that found in a six-ounce cup of coffee.[176] It has the added advantage that it is easy to transport, does not increase the need to go to the bathroom, and can be used in extreme cold and extreme heat.[177]

Companies are also investigating the use of gum for introducing medicine into the body, as opposed to syrups, pills, or patches. Currently, gum companies already include healthful ingredients such as green tea and calcium in their gum recipes, but scientists are researching the potential for delivering medicine directly to the bloodstream. A Danish study noted that cheeks are extremely effective for absorbing medications, and that participants ingested nearly three times the amount of antihistamine through chewing gum, as opposed to taking a pill that has to be digested.[178] Despite these technological advances in chewing gum, manufacturers have still not found a solution to proper disposal, and urban sidewalks around the world are littered with it. This problem was recognized as early as 1939, when New York City Mayor LaGuardia wrote a letter to the heads of the major chewing gum companies about the problem of cleaning up the sidewalks. He complained that it cost the city literally hundreds of thousands of dollars a year and implored them to take part in a "campaign of education" for teaching proper gum disposal techniques. A PR campaign was initiated by city hall, and slogans such as "Chew it but don't strew it," "Don't be a gum-bell," and "Don't gum up the works" were all considered. Beech-Nut Packing Company and William Wrigley Jr. Company agreed to print various notices on their gum wrappers about the mayor's program and continued to encourage proper disposal.[179] Social etiquette writers of the 1950s suggested, often in vain, that gum chewers save their wrappers to keep others from having to step in their mess.[180] It became such a problem in Singapore that the country banned the import, manufacture, and sale of chewing gum beginning in 1992. Although the law was relaxed in 2002 to allow for the use of nicotine gum by prescription, the government still enforces the penalty of 10,000 Singapore dollars (the equivalent of $5,500 U.S. dollars) and a year in jail.[181] However, a British company may have solved this long-term disposal problem. The University of Bristol and its associated company Revolymer have announced the invention of "Clean Gum," a product made to be easily removed from hair, clothing, and sidewalks. This nonadhesive product is water degradable and generally disappears within twenty-four hours.[182]

Other research has focused on the potential benefits of chewing gum. In addition to the earlier investigations that demonstrated that gum chewing reduced tension,[183] more recent studies have shown that sugar-free gums that contain sorbitol and xylitol can increase salivation and reduce cavities by neutralizing the acids in the mouth that develop after eating.[184] Scientists have also demonstrated that gum chewing may improve memory under certain conditions. In a study conducted in the United Kingdom, psychologists found that people who chewed gum throughout long-term and short-term memory tests had scores that were 35 percent higher than people who did not.[185] This may be explained by the recent finding of Japanese researchers that when people chew, brain activity increases in the hippocampus, which is an area important for memory. Although speculative, some feel this might be because insulin, which the body produces when it is expecting food, may help aid in memory. Another explanation may be that chewing increases the body's heart rate, which would improve the delivery of oxygen to the brain, and thus improve memory.[186] However, subsequent studies demonstrated that chewing gum did not improve memory under most conditions and that these earlier claims should be viewed with caution.[187]

The Chicle Industry Today

Great fortunes still exist in the synthetic chewing gum industry. When William Wrigley III died in 1999, his estate was worth over $3 billion.[188] Today, William Wrigley IV, great-grandson of the Wrigley chewing gum company founder, is consistently in the top fifty on the Forbes 400 list of richest Americans.[189] This is not surprising in light of the fact that, as of 2006, the gum sector has grown 7 percent over three years and is worth more than $19 billion annually. However, natural chicle-based chewing gum production has been downsized to a boutique industry, based primarily in Japan and Korea, as well as Italy and Mexico.[190]

By the 1980s the natural chicle industry was all but abandoned. Small cooperatives had formed, organized along the ejido or shared-land boundaries, and chicleros from the same villages would pool their collected chicle and then split the profits. By the early 1990s these had virtually collapsed because of poor management and the fact that many individuals were sorely underpaid under the pooling arrangement. However, in 1993–94, the Secretaría del Desarrollo Social (Department of Social Development) arranged for some seed money to fund a small number of cooperatives and to bring back the chicle extraction on a small scale. Eventually, a group of nine cooperatives was formed, which allowed each chiclero to earn his wages on the basis of how much chicle he brought in individually. This became known as the Plan Piloto Chiclero.[191] Started in 1994, the idea behind this program was to establish a central production base that protected the workers by negotiating fair prices for their harvest and used transparency in managing finances of the cooperative. Today there are some forty cooperatives in the Yucatán organized into a marketing consortium representing more than fifteen hundred workers who collect chicle, honey, and hardwoods.[192] Although once a major source of employment, today's chicle extraction industry represents a limited opportunity for the contemporary Maya. Without an increased need for chicle gum base, this is not likely to improve.

There are a small number of buyers that purchase chicle at high prices and sell it to a limited market of consumers looking to buy a "natural" product. Because the demand for chicle is so small today, overtapping is no longer an issue.[193] The methods used to tap chicle today directly parallel those used in the late 1890s, although the transport of the processed bricks to the manufacturing plants has certainly modernized. The latex that is collected today is of an extremely high quality. Because of the limited market, the chicleros have realized that it is in their best interest to provide a superior product to ensure that buyers will continue their contracts.[194]

Verve, Inc., based in Providence, Rhode Island, is currently the only company in the United States to sell gum with chicle included in its gum base, sold under the "Glee Gum" brand name (fig. 3.4). Previously, a company known as Wild Things, Inc. sold the chicle-based "Jungle Gum" out of Gainesville, Florida; however, they have since gone out of business. In addition to retail distribution at stores such as Trader Joe's and Whole Foods, Verve also sells naturally flavored and colored chewing gum (as well as a "Make Your Own Chewing Gum Kit") online via its Web site, www.gleegum.com. Currently, their unprocessed chicle comes from the consortium of chicle cooperatives in Quintana Roo, Mexico. However, as the consortium is not yet capable of processing chicle into gum base, Verve, Inc. has it processed in Europe. Despite this cost and inconvenience, they choose to work directly with the chicleros because of their conviction that tapping chicle is an important part of a sustainable income strategy for the forest dwellers of the area. They sell roughly two million packs of Glee Gum annually, but because there is such a relatively small demand for, and difficulty with supply and processing,

Figure 3.4. Glee Gum, the only natural chicle-based gum currently made in the Americas. (Photograph by Jenny Lederer. Image courtesy of Verve, Inc)

organic gum ingredients, there is little incentive for other companies to offer organic gum.[195] However, recently the Consorcio Cooperativo de Productores y Exportadores en Forestería (Cooperative Consortium of Forestry Producers and Exporters) has gained certification to create an organic chicle-based gum known as Chicza they are exporting to Europe on a small scale.[196]

Discussion

The history of chicle has come full circle from being used on a small scale by the ancient Maya and Aztec to being used on a small scale by modern consumers. The boom-and-bust economy perpetrated by North American companies and complicit Central American governments resulted in an unsustainable industry that ultimately left thousands of indigenous laborers underpaid and eventually unemployed. It also resulted in a system in which most chicleros were primarily concerned with obtaining the maximum quantity of chicle, at the cost of the health of the trees and the quality of the latex. Like all extractive industries, if not kept in check, its success results in its own downfall. Despite the recent examples of hardwood and chicle, Mesoamerica is on its way to repeating this history once again through its newest extractive industry: tourism. The parallels between the growth of the chicle industry and tourism in this region warrant comparison, as the mega-resorts threaten to disrupt the local peoples and destroy the beautiful landscape of the region, while also providing the backbone of the local economy. Much like some ecotourism programs, today's small-scale chicle business provides consumers with an option to support a more sustainable industry. By purchasing chicle-based gum such as Glee Gum and/or other natural, Fair Trade, or organic products like eggs, meat, produce, coffee, and chocolate, consumers are able to vote with their dollars to support these kinds of smaller companies and healthier products. Additionally, if there is enough demand for the products, they are indirectly supporting small-scale and indigenous labor markets that can provide long-term employment. It is this kind of extractive industry that can result in long-term employment with better wages, a healthier forest, a better product for the consumer, and a greater awareness of the impact of our consumer choices.

4

THE CHICLEROS

> To the chiclero, death is but sport, and commonplace. A word, a foul
> expression, anything, in their eyes is enough justification to take a human
> life. If these men are violent, they nevertheless are in many ways good
> men. . . . a school of cutthroats hardened by the fight for survival in the
> jungle, where their foes were not only nature but every man who could
> not be counted a sure friend.
> —Michel Peissel, a French writer and ethnographer observing chicleros in
>   the Yucatán Peninsula in the early 1960s[1]

> I worked eighteen years in chicle and came out with nothing but a pair
> of pants.
> —A Guatemalan chiclero summing up his experience in the chicle
>   industry[2]

At the turn of the century, the territories of Quintana Roo, Mexico, northern
Belize, and Petén of Guatemala were very much like the old and wild west. They
were sparsely populated and the government had little control of the region. As
discussed in chapter 3, the Maya of Mexico had been fighting for their lands
and freedom since the 1800s.[3] The life and work of the chiclero—far removed
from the reach of the law, unscrutinized, and mostly unsupervised—attracted
criminals on the run and those shunned by their indigenous villages, but also
independent-minded workers from around the world. The chicle camps could be
anarchic and violent places, but many chicleros brought their wives and children,
avoided trouble, and simply made their living in the solitude of the forest. The
legends of the wild and lawless life of the chiclero, like the legends of the North
American cowboy, tended toward the vivid exaggerations that eager audiences
back in civilization preferred. Paydays could be wild with drink and fighting, but
mostly chicleros, like the cowboys, worked hard and solitarily for their living.

The Influence of the Henequen and Lumber Industries

The chicle industry was born out of the depression of the henequen industry that dominated in the state of Yucatán starting in the 1820s. Henequen is a natural fiber that is extracted from along the length of the leaves of the agave plant (*Agave fourcroydes*). The crop was exported almost exclusively to the United States and was used primarily to make binding twine for the agricultural industry, rope, and rugs. The monocrop was grown on haciendas, and more than half of the state was employed in the industry.[4] Many of the *henequeneros* had lost their communal agricultural lands to the hacienda owners and were dependent on them for employment and food through debt peonage.[5] While the workers suffered from poor pay and oppressive working conditions, the hacienda owners achieved great wealth and paved the streets, built mansions, and brought electricity and horse-drawn streetcars to the capitol city of Mérida. By the year 1900, the United States was importing eighty-one million kilos of henequen from Yucatán State. In 1902, the American financier J. P. Morgan organized a merger of several major farm-harvesting equipment manufacturers into the International Harvesting Company. As the largest producer of binding twine, IHC was able to control prices as the buyer of 80 percent of Yucatán's henequen crop. Morgan lowered the price of henequen so much that he nearly bankrupted the industry. By the end of World War I, Yucatán's economy had virtually collapsed from years of low prices. In the 1930s, North American manufacturers began to import the stronger sisal fiber from plantations in Africa and Java, and the henequen industry continued to decline. By 1937 President Lázaro Cárdenas reverted the majority of hacienda land back to ejido land, in the hopes that local peoples would be able to grow their own food again.[6]

During the waxing and waning of henequen prices in the late 1800s, the *hacenderos* (hacienda owners) sought to expand and diversify their holdings by moving to the eastern half of the peninsula where they knew that the forests had rich holdings of valuable hardwoods and forest products. In 1876, Ramón Ancona founded the Compañía Agrícola and extended his land holdings into Quintana Roo. This land was then acquired by two Yucatecos, Eusebio Escalente and Raymundo Cámara, in 1897 and converted to the Compañia del Cuyo y Anexas. The Bank of London and Mexico also funded the Compañía Colonizadora de la

Costa Oriental de Yucatán, which acquired four thousand square miles of land near the coast.[7]

About this same time, chicle extraction was introduced into the Petén region of Guatemala, which was also sparsely populated and suffering from a listless economy. Most Peteneros had worked as loggers, *milperos* (corn farmers), *huleros* (rubber tappers), and cowboys, all of which were part of a weak economic market. Because the region provided little financial gain compared with the coffee and banana harvests of other areas of Guatemala, the state took little interest, and most chicle and logging extraction was minor in the early days.[8] Since the mid-1600s, Belize had been producing an extractive commodity, small-scale harvesting of *Haematoxylon campechianum*, or logwood, which was used in Europe as a dye. By the early 1700s, the lumber industry had developed large-scale trade in mahogany, which remained active into the 1960s. Chicle, however, was a relatively unimportant commodity at first. Although Belize first exported chicle around 1866, it was likely a supply smuggled in from Guatemala.[9] The chicle industry was not truly established until the 1920s, and even then it was only with encouragement from a Mr. Hummel, the forestry officer of British Honduras. By 1934, he had persuaded private parties to create a forty-thousand-acre sapodilla plantation. However, by 1928 it was clear that the chicle tree was not suited for plantation-style harvesting, and the project was abandoned. The land was then taken over by the Tropical Plant Research Foundation, led by J. S. Karling, to conduct a five-year study on tapping. By the end of the study period, that project had been similarly abandoned, and Belize never contributed more than a small percentage of the latex supply for the United States.[10]

The Buildup of Infrastructure and the Labor Force

Once the land was acquired for exploiting chicle and hardwoods like mahogany, the infrastructure for these industries needed to be developed. This meant building narrow-gauge railways, roads and paths, permanent housing for camp managers, chicle and wood processing centers, huts for workers, and corrals for mules and horses. As the regions where sapodilla trees were abundant were sparsely populated areas, companies also had to bring in workers from elsewhere. This followed the tradition of importing cheap and temporary workers for the henequen industry. During labor shortages, Mexican hacienda owners imported criminals from all over the country, brought Huastec Indians from central Mexico, and rounded up Yaqui Indians who had been rebelling in Sonora.[11] They also looked afar for workers. In 1905, an English slave trader by the name of Myers brought approximately one thousand Koreans to Yucatán. Although working for the Mexican hacienda owners, he presented himself to the Korean government as a merchant looking for workers for the sugarcane plantations in Hawaii. Since many Koreans had been immigrating there and Myers offered a cash bonus for signing a four-year contract, he had no problem recruiting workers. Instead of delivering them to Hawaii, however, he diverted them to the port at Progreso just outside of Mérida and sold them to the henequen hacienda owners. They worked as virtual slaves until their contracts expired in 1909. Few of them could afford the return fare to Korea, and many of them remained as laborers in the Yucatán Peninsula well into the twentieth century.[12] The chiclero workforce in Quintana Roo was thus made up of a mishmash of criminals, local Maya, former henequen workers including Koreans, as well as migrants from Veracruz, the Caribbean islands, and Central America.[13] Although the total number of chicleros in Petén was estimated to be as many as a thousand workers by the 1920s, it is unclear how many of them were foreigners, as their number has probably always been underestimated. This is in part because the Guatemalan government failed to keep records before the 1930s, and because labor contractors were expected to pay a fee to the government for each foreigner it employed. It is also difficult to estimate the total number of workers in Guatemala, as many of them may have worked only part-time or for a few seasons and then dropped out.[14] We do know, however, that Belizeans (often of Lebanese descent) and Mexicans were frequently employed in the chicle extraction of Petén.[15]

In 1910, the labor force in Mexico consisted of a mere three thousand chicleros and less than a thousand in Petén. However, by World War II, chicle extraction was the most important industry in the Yucatán and the third most important in Guatemala, employing over forty thousand people.[16] Companies constructed numerous airstrips by felling forests and allowing low-growing shrubs to form a grassy runway. Contractors created small operations of around three hundred chicleros in remote areas. This included camps in eastern Chiapas, where Mexican pilots flew single-motored planes with roughly twelve hundred pounds of chicle latex without radio communications for delivery into Tenosinque, Tabasco.[17] Overall, wages were relatively low, but as manufacturers recognized chicle tapping as a skilled labor, chicleros were among the highest paid of native workers.[18] In a study that compared chicleros with other laborers in Yucatán, they often earned more and their children were better educated. In Petén they were sometimes able to work their way into positions as foremen or merchant-contractors, allowing them to pay to educate their children as teachers or professionals. Chicleros were often seen as being free with their money, as is reflected in the saying "El chiclero no pide vuleto" (Chicleros do not ask for change).[19]

Daily Life of the Chiclero

When the rainy season started in June, chicleros from inland and coastal villages migrated in small groups to the chicle camps (arriving by airplane, mule, or on foot), sometimes bringing their families with them (fig. 4.1).[20] Experienced chicleros occasionally brought friends and sons as new recruits, working with them to teach them the basic skills needed for harvesting independently.[21] Maya and other local chicleros tended to be more careful in their tapping techniques and adhered to the regional norms, whereas without proper guidance, migrant chicleros might be more likely to overtap the sapodillas.[22]

Individual camps usually consisted of twelve to twenty workers and when possible included one female cook for every ten workers.[23] Chicleros brought few personal items with them, as company stores provided equipment such as machetes, canvas collection bags, spurs for climbing trees, molds, paddles, and cooking pots, which camp managers deducted from their future earnings (see figs. 4.2–4.4). Although they spent some time in the more permanent camps that were maintained by their managers, most of their days were spent in the jungle collecting. Their jungle camps were generally made up of a few temporary pole-and-thatch shacks, a table made of scrap wood, and hammocks (fig. 4.2).[24] A central hut acted as a storage and cooking area and included large metal cauldrons for processing the latex. Because their camp was filled with valuable chicle bricks and supplies, chicleros usually kept at least one gun to protect the camp from thieves, as well as for hunting. Although some of the larger camps included female cooks, most chicleros woke up before dawn and made their own food, usually

Figure 4.1. A chiclero eating with his family in a camp in Yucatán. (Photograph courtesy of Macduff Everton)

Figure 4.2. A chicle camp with a small shelter and a cooking area, 1971. (Photograph courtesy of Macduff Everton)

consisting of beans and tortillas. Food and supplies were typically purchased at the chicleros' expense and brought to the camps on a weekly basis by mule. This ensured that they were continually building up more debt and kept them working. One study of chicleros in Guatemala demonstrated that two-thirds of chicleros never earned enough from their chicle extraction to pay back their debts.[25]

The workday began before dawn. The chicleros found that the best flow of latex occurred in the early morning, although they usually tapped trees until the late afternoon and in all weather.[26] Harvesting of chicle was focused during the rainy season[27] (generally from July to February), and they spent long days in the forest seeking out sapodilla trees that had not already been tapped. They often worked in groups of two to three men, staying within whistling distance of each other so as not to get lost.[28] Chicleros sometimes left individualized marks on the trunks of the sapodilla to help them keep track of their tappings. Preferably, the trees were left untouched for five years between cuttings to ensure that they would continue to be fruitful. Once a new sapodilla was found, they had to clear the vegetation around the base of the trunk.[29] Chicleros often tested a tree for flow levels by placing a small cut into the bark. If the tree was viable, the chiclero would tie metal spikes to his shoes and use ropes known as *cabos* to climb. Ascending from the base of the tree, he would slash the length of the tree in a zigzag pattern with a machete in a process known as *picado* (pricking) (see fig. 1.1). Back on the ground, the chiclero placed a large canvas bag called a *recogedera* at the base of the trunk beneath the cuts. The bags were left in place to collect the oozing resin that ran down the channels hacked into the bark. On a good morning, an experienced chiclero might be able to tap eight trees. The chiclero would return later that day or the next to collect the full bags and take them back to camp using a large sack known as a *chibo* and a tumpline (a rope that they would tie across their forehead to carry their loads).[30] Trees had the strongest flow of latex at 6:00 a.m., particularly when it had rained the night before. However, a heavy daytime shower could wash away the chicle, or wind and sun could cause it to dry out and stick to the trunk of the tree.[31]

After enough resin was collected (usually once a week), the chicleros would remove it from the collection bags and place it into a large metal *olla* (pot) on a wood fire, and stir it regularly with a long wooden paddle (fig. 4.3). They would boil it slowly and stir it continuously (as it scorches like milk) until the material

Figure 4.3. A chiclero boiling chicle to remove moisture and bacteria. (Photograph courtesy of Macduff Everton)

Figure 4.4. Chicleros preparing to pour chicle into a wooden mold known as a *marqueta*. (Photograph courtesy of Macduff Everton)

coagulated, decreasing the natural moisture content and killing bacteria. During the cooling process, chicleros aerated the latex by whipping it like cake batter, and then laid out a canvas and rectangular wooden molds, or *marquetas* (fig. 4.4). The mold and canvas were wiped down with soap or detergent to keep the chicle from sticking. Once removed from the mold, the chicle formed a hard brick weighing around 9 kg (or roughly 20 lbs), and the chicleros stamped their initials into it.[32] Cooking of the chicle was also advantageous for production as it resulted in the preservation of the rubbery state for up to five years, permitting foreign manufacturers to store large quantities for long periods of time.[33]

Camp supervisors would intermittently arrive at the camps to weigh the blocks of chicle and assess the need for supplies and equipment. The supervisor had a direct interest in the quality and quantity of the chicle produced, as it determined his seasonal income.[34] He acted as a kind of intermediary, setting the prices paid to chicleros and then providing the raw resource to the manufacturers. He also calculated the earnings of a chiclero entirely on an individual's production of chicle, which he paid out at the end of the season.[35] The unit of transaction was five 9 kg blocks, known as a *quintal*.[36] In order to keep up with the company's production quotas, chicleros sometimes included the inferior resin of other trees, or placed rocks or sand in the blocks of chicle to increase the weight.[37] In response to the problem, camp managers began testing for impurities and paid lower prices for poorer grades of chicle, causing the practice to be greatly reduced.[38] Camp managers had their own ways of cheating, duping their workers by short-weighing the chicle blocks and underpaying them.[39]

When the chicleros in Petén, northern Belize, and the interior of Quintana Roo had processed a large supply of chicle, the bricks were loaded onto a railroad truck, mule, airplane, or boat and brought to the east coast of Quintana Roo. By the 1930s, there were five main narrow-gauge rail lines in Quintana Roo that transported workers, chicle, hardwoods, and supplies between the interior and the coast, includ-ing a 168 km section from Santa Cruz de Bravo to Peto, a 150 km rail from Santa Cruz to Bacalar, a section from Bacalar to Payo Obispo (now Chetumal), a 15 km stretch from Payo Obispo to Ichpaatun, a 40 km segment from Puerto Morelos to Santa María (with a 15 km branch to Solferino and a 50 km section to Puerto Juárez), and a 57 km rail from Vigía Chico to Santa Cruz Bravo.[40] The railroads were built at great cost to the government, due to the difficulty of penetrating the dense forest.[41]

Belgian M. Paul Decauville designed the narrow-gauge rail lines that were used on plantations for harvesting crops from around the world. They were specifically designed to make them relatively easy to install right onto the ground or upon a flat raised bed and could be moved as the locations of harvesting areas changed. The narrow and delicate design made them more appropriate for animal-powered versus engine-powered trains. In India, elephants were used to pull the carts, while in Mexico they relied on harnessed horses and mules that walked alongside the tracks (fig. 4.5).[42] Camps were placed approximately every 10 km or so, which was roughly the distance that an animal could carry a load before becoming fatigued.[43] Once the chicle stores had been brought to the coast of Quintana Roo, they were then collected by the transport ships used by corporations such as the United Fruit Company and distributed to U.S. and Canadian manufacturers.[44]

Figure 4.5. Chicleros riding on a horse-drawn train near Puerto Morelos, Quintana Roo. (Photograph courtesy of Jorge Sánchez)

In addition to collecting and processing chicle daily, camp workers were responsible for maintaining the railways by repairing the rail bed and regularly making and replacing parts such as wooden ties and metal nails. They had to maintain the tools of their trade as well, keeping their machetes sharp, their collection bags and cooking cauldrons clean of resin, and making sure that their ropes and spikes were in good condition.[45] Workers were expected to wash their own clothes, chop their own wood, and rarely had days of rest or time to attend church.[46] Additionally, they were required to keep the encroaching forest cleared on either side of the railway tracks or trails used for transport, and they were frequently wounded by venomous snakes and poisonous plants and trees in the process.[47] Some chicleros also reported that cooking the chicle caused damage to the eyes, particularly after several hours.[48]

Disease-carrying insects regularly bit workers, resulting in malaria and chiclero ulcer. Chiclero ulcer, also known as *cutaneous leishmaniasis*, is a swelling to exposed areas, usually the nose, lips, or ears. It is caused by the bite of the black fly (*Lutzomya olmeca*, also known as *mosca chiclera* in Spanish), which resides only in tropical forests in Central America.[49] The disease occurs almost exclusively during the rainy season and is found predominantly on animals (such as monkeys, dogs, deer, and peccaries) and chicleros or other workers who spend time in the remote jungle. If left unchecked, it results in a lesion that eats away the skin, much like leprosy.[50] A 1930s study estimated that nearly 10 percent of all chicleros endured this tropical disease, and many of them were permanently disfigured with scars or mutilated noses, lips, and ears.[51] There was no one treatment for the lesions, although remedies ranged from the placement of penicillin powder, toothpaste, alcohol, gasoline, papaya, and armadillo fat on the wound.[52] Prehistoric populations likely suffered from the disease as well. J. Eric S. Thompson hypothesized that pre-Columbian artists who depicted dogs with mutilated ears may have been portraying them with chiclero ulcer. He went on to argue that the portrayal of lacerated ears in Mesoamerican art in general may be explained by the common presence of chiclero ulcer in prehistory.[53]

The chicle camps were portable, and chicleros were repeatedly required to move the location of the interim camps to keep them within reasonable walking distances to tappable trees.[54] The rudimentary shelters offered little protection from the elements, which included heavy rains and brutal sun. They always had to keep an eye out for water sources, but as most chicleros were unable to afford water-purifying tablets or filters, they frequently had to drink polluted water. They regularly endured snakebites, and told tall tales about snakes, sometimes trying to convince newcomers that snakes could sting you with their tails or chase after you by rolling like a hoop.[55] They experienced machete accidents and falls from trees on a regular basis and often developed skin disorders. Some companies encouraged them to use the durable black chechem (*Metopium brownei* (Jacq.) Urb.) wood for making railroad ties, which has a harmful sap that could cause blistering and extreme swelling when it came in contact with skin.[56] As the companies provided no medical care to the chicleros while they were in the bush, workers relied on traditional remedies for curing snakebites and fevers, and sometimes chewed herbs that caused colic but kept them from getting amoebic dysentery.[57]

After long days, workers occasionally got disoriented or lost in the jungle, forcing others to try to locate them with a series of calls, whistles, or gun shots into the air. Chicleros often reported that spirits or goblins roamed the jungle, stealing their equipment, spilling their collection bags, or sometimes causing them to become lost. Some would even create jungle shrines with offerings of black wax candles and black pepper for protection.[58]

In addition to the natural difficulties they faced in the jungle, the dangerous human element within the permanent chicle camps compounded the struggle of daily life. The company store provided workers with a limited diet of mostly beans and tortillas that had to be supplemented by hunting. Chicleros preferred the meat of wild turkeys, peccaries, or deer,[59] although they also ate dove, iguana, gopher, and monkey. They had almost no access to fresh fruits and vegetables in the permanent camps, as any gardens were generally limited to use by the managers. Sometimes they would introduce citrus and banana trees near their remote camps to provide some fruit in their diets.[60] During medical studies of residents at the Santa María camp in the northeastern corner of Quintana Roo, 20 percent (26 out of 130) of them exhibited anemia, reflecting their poor diet, parasites, and the presence of diseases like malaria.[61]

The overall combination of poor working and living conditions frustrated chicleros, who had little recourse for negotiating with their employers other than through uprisings. These seemed to do little to help their cause, as evidenced by the violent uprising in 1929 that made international news. The result was that the Mexican government sent troops to stop the rebellion,[62] and within just a few years many of those same camps had been abandoned and workers had to move elsewhere.[63] In general, laborers were without steady employment in the off-season between March and May or when waiting for a delayed rainy season. Although sometimes able to find an odd job, the chicleros who did not return to their villages were dependent on contractors continuing to provide food and shelter during the dry season. This regularly resulted in chicleros running up additional debts above those already incurred during the working season, forcing them to be bound to the contractor in a kind of debt servitude.[64]

Many corn farmers (*milperos*) gave up their agricultural practices to become chicleros because they believed that they would make more money. The height of the chicle season correlated with the rainy season, which meant that the agricultural fields were left unattended when they most needed protection from pests, as well as harvesting and storage. This resulted in major grain shortages, which the Mexican government attempted to correct by ordering all milpas to be maintained. Since the men were in the jungles for months at a time, it was the women who were left behind to keep up the milpas. Because women already had the responsibility of running the households, caring for the children, and cooking all of the food, they usually lacked the time and training to watch over the fields.[65] The result was that the price of basic staples such as corn and beans went up for everyone,[66] and most of the farmers made less or no more money than before.

Chiclero = Criminal

Outsiders have often viewed chicleros negatively, in part because they were indigenous laborers, but also because of issues of alcoholism, gambling, prostitution, violence, and even murder within the camps.[67] Local peoples generally feared the chicleros and considered them to be one of the dangers of the jungle, as many were rumored to be ex-convicts, Maya rebels, and criminals on the lam.[68] One reporter from the United States observed that, "One may find it stated in serious American archaeological reports that all the fugitives from Latin-American justice end in Quintana Roo chicle trails."[69] Although many of the accounts of their behavior have likely been exaggerated, these fears were not totally unfounded. Before starting a tapping season, and after receiving pay advances, chicleros often went on drinking binges and spent much of their pay on drinks for themselves and their companions. Similarly, after long periods of remote living in the forest and conducting months of solitary, dangerous, and dulling work, chicleros might arrive in local towns with pockets full of money and a need to blow off steam. Public drunkenness and other disruptive behavior colored public opinion of chicleros, and they were seen as people to be avoided.[70]

It does seem that violent behavior was prevalent in chiclero culture, at least before the 1970s. A French writer named Michel Peissel, who walked the length of the coast of Quintana Roo in the early 1960s, came across numerous chicleros during his adventure. In one encounter he explained, "He told me he had once been a chiclero but had abandoned that rough life to live on the coast. I was surprised that a young man like Miguel could stand the solitude of the coast and be satisfied with living completely alone. It was only later that I learned that, involved in a fight, Miguel had killed a man, and now considered it preferable, like many other chicleros, to live in unpopulated areas."[71] In another account he described that during the 1950s, the chicleros of Quintana Roo were divided up into two gangs that were led by El Cawamo ("Big-Headed Turtle") and La Tortuga ("The Tortoise"). El Cawamo had a reputation for seeking out chicleros that were from La Tortuga and killing them for their chicle supply. He was eventually attacked by La Tortuga's men, dragged twelve miles to a boat, taken to a prison in Cozumel, and killed the next day.[72] The Santa María camp in Quintana Roo (now Leona Vicario), at one time the largest chicle-processing area in the Yucatán Peninsula, had a reputation for being particularly brutal. It was the inland termination of a 40 km long narrow-gauge railroad that led to the coast at Puerto Morelos, and included a large two-story clapboard house for the camp managers, shacks for the workers, and a large chicle-processing area. Funded with money from the Bank of London and Mexico, and constructed in 1900, it was part of the Compañía Colonizadora enterprise.[73] Even in the late 1950s and 1960s, it was reputed for "the worst murders, brawls, and hair-raising, authentic cases of crime in all of Mexico." Toward the end of the season when the chicleros had been paid, thousands of men would come to the headquarters to dance, have sex with prostitutes, and drink rum. On many Sunday mornings following the all-night parties, two or three dead bodies were reportedly found outside the central building at the camp.[74]

Nonetheless, violence was not inevitable, and many chicleros dealt with tension by simply avoiding it. One recorded case occurred in the Petén region where a camp had a mixture of Mexicans and Guatemalans working together. Tensions began to develop when the camp cook began serving more food to the Mexicans, which eventually led to a fight during a card game. Some workers simply avoided each other after that, but the camp manager began having trouble keeping a few of the workers calm. One day, he awoke to find that all of the Mexicans had left without a word and resettled their camp several kilometers away.[75]

In addition to their violent reputations, chicleros were criticized for being promiscuous vectors of venereal disease. Thomas Gann, an anthropologist and explorer of the Maya region observed, "Even among the mixed breeds of British Honduras, they [venereal diseases] are comparatively rare, notwithstanding the fact that these natives have come much in contact with people of many other races, especially of late years with Mexican Chicleros, nearly all of whom are affected with venereal diseases in one form or another."[76] G. C. Shattuck, a medical doctor who visited many of the chicle camps in Yucatán in the early 1930s found that roughly 46 out of every 1,000 Maya people in the peninsula tested positive for syphilis. However, within the notorious camp of Santa María, he found a surprisingly low rate of syphilis and gonorrhea. When he examined 130 of the chicleros who met with him at the camp, only one adult male tested positive and exhibited both gonorrhea and syphilis.[77] Although Shattuck suspected that the local population had a kind of resistance to syphilis, the chicleros may have been using a local remedy that infused the root of the cocolmeca plant (*Milleria quinqueflora* L.) with a piece of the quiebrahacha bush (*Stylogyne lateriflora* (Sw.) Mez) into a drink.[78]

Camp cooks were usually single or divorced women working away from home in an all-male camp, and outsiders generally saw them as "loose" and viewed them with disdain. "[T]hey [chicleros] sometimes fight over the cook who is almost always a single woman and a whore. It is rare when the cook does not sleep with the men for money. The men sometimes fight over her because two of them may want to sleep with her at the same time." In reality, camp managers made a concerted effort to avoid having prostitutes or "indecent" women in the camps. It was the norm for chicleros to treat female cooks with respect, and they were more likely to compete over her for food and attention than sex.[79]

Despite the chicleros' overall fierce reputation, when foreigners actually visited chicle camps they often stated that chicleros welcomed the company of strangers, were highly intelligent and perceptive, and were generous with their supplies to guests.[80] By the early 1970s chicleros were generally considered to be less violent and more of them were bringing their families with them to the remote camps (see fig. 4.1). Wives and children helped to fix up the temporary houses to make them more hospitable, such as providing table cloths and laying down clay and soft limestone to make a smooth floor. Children were expected to help with collecting firewood, cooking, and carrying water from the nearby cenotes (karstic sinkholes).[81] However, by this time there was little work to be had, as overtapping of the sapodilla trees had greatly reduced the supply, and most of the chewing gum industry was using the cheaper synthetic materials to make chewing gum.[82] Chicleros were forced to go farther into the forest to find untapped trees, and they were paid the same wages year after year, though their expenses continued to increase. Small cooperatives had formed in the 1980s, but due to poor management these had collapsed. The chicle extraction industry was all but abandoned, and the overwhelming majority of chicleros had to find alternative sources of income such as fishing and corn farming.[83]

In 1994, in an attempt to serve the boutique natural chewing gum industry, a new cooperative known as Plan Piloto Chiclero was formed in Quintana Roo to give individual chicleros more control over their earnings. Companies like Verve, Inc. have attempted to work directly with the chicleros to obtain chicle latex and provide them with a higher income.[84] A few former chicleros in Quintana Roo have also recognized the economic potential of small-scale tourism and are developing private sites with swimming cenotes, zip-lines through the jungle, horse-powered flatbed trains, and replicas of chiclero camps.[85] Nonetheless, an industry that once employed thousands has dwindled, and the actual collection of chicle is all but a lost art rarely passed from father to son.

Chicleros and Their Role in Archaeology

Chicleros have been accused of being many things—hardworking drunks, murderers, and rapists—but we should not forget that chicleros were also naturalists, advisors, and guides to archaeologists. In general, they have an excellent working knowledge of forest plants and usually know the names and habits of wildlife.[86] They often know which plants are edible or provide water and even make wild teas.[87] Additionally, they can pinpoint water sources and other natural features such as cenotes, *rejolladas* (natural soil-filled depressions), and caves. During their daily explorations for untapped sapodilla trees, chicleros came across numerous archaeological sites under the cover of the jungle. Archaeologists have taken advantage of this knowledge of the locations of ancient settlements and have hired them as guides for nearly a century. As archaeologist Frans Blom once said, "chewing gum and Maya archaeology are closely related," implying that archaeologists got to know much of the Maya area through the chiclero trails and with the help of chiclero guides. Archaeologist and photographer Giles Healy noted in 1947 that when the demand for chicle grew during World War II and chicle extraction spread, local companies began to build airfields.[88] When they did, even more ruins were discovered in the previously impenetrable jungle. Some of the most important Maya sites ever discovered were found with the assistance of chiclero guides along their jungle trails.

In 1923, Sylvanus Morley initiated a large study in which he would attempt to determine the locations of the major sites of the Maya region. He was (rightfully) concerned that the chiclero paths that had opened the forest to foreign explorers for the first time could be lost if a substitute were found for chicle and the industry went into decline. He lamented that the jungle paths were only visible with constant use and that with the eventual loss of the chicle trails would come "the consequent loss to knowledge of many important Maya sites." For sixteen years he organized expeditions through the Carnegie Institution of Washington DC, and with the aid of chiclero guides uncovered forty-three sites. He found the major site of Uaxactún after offering a reward of twenty-five dollars in gold to chicleros who could take him to new sites that contained inscribed monuments.[89] Ultimately, as a result of this project, he was also able to produce the first accurate map of the northern Petén and southern Yucatán Peninsula.[90]

Chiclero Francisco Morales first discovered the site of Calakmul in Campeche when he was cutting a trail through the forest. In 1932, C. L. Lundell found out about the ruins while working for eight months in the region as a botanist for the American Chicle Development Company.[91] The discovery caught the attention of archaeologist Sylvanus Morley, who spent two weeks mapping and studying the ancient city. Soon after he informed a reporter: "Calakmul exceeds our expectations. It contains the tremendous total of one hundred three stelae with sculptured figures and hieroglyphs, many more sculptured monuments than any Maya city hitherto known."[92] To this day, Calakmul contains the highest number of stelae ever found in the Maya area and is considered to be one of the most significant sites known.[93] During the same exploratory trip with chiclero guides, Lundell found twelve other sites in southern Campeche and northern Guatemala, including Bomba, Multun, and Nohoxna. Each of the sites was briefly mapped and photographed, and all data was turned over to the Carnegie Institution of Washington DC.[94]

For several seasons, starting in 1933, the Carnegie Institution sent archaeologists Karl Ruppert, John Denison Jr., and J. P. O'Neill to document new sites in Campeche, Quintana Roo, and northern Petén. They learned that it was advantageous to work during the chicle season so that they could interview chicleros about the locations of ruins. However, as this was during the rainy season, they decided instead to send a local native who could travel with the chicleros to the sites and then guide the expedition once the rainy season was over. They often used the flatbed rail trucks and mules of the chicle camps to transport personnel and equipment, and in some cases stayed in abandoned chicle camps on their way out to sites.[95] Using a guide, they were able to relocate the site of Nohoxna that Lundell had reported the year before. Over their twelve-day stay they found several new buildings and stelae and completed a map of the site. However, on their return, they realized that the sites of Nohoxna and Naachtun, which had already been studied by Sylvanus Morley in 1923, were one and the same place. Morley had been taken there by chiclero Olfonso Ovando, who had first encountered the remote city six years earlier. It is still one of the most isolated and least-known sites in northern Petén, although recently researcher Kathryn Reese-Taylor has been revisiting the ruins. Her work has demonstrated that it contains over forty stelae and large public architecture with influence from the nearby Rio Bec area. The texts indicate it was a powerful Classic-period site within the Calakmul sphere, and according to a stela at Tikal was conquered by the Tikal kingdom in AD 486. By the Late Classic period the site was fortified by a thirteen-foot-tall wall and eventually suffered a decline during the ninth century.[96]

In 1946, local chicleros led Carl Frey and John Bourne to the site of Bonampak in Chiapas. While there, they mapped several of the buildings, although the heavy foliage caused them to miss a structure with murals. A year later, Giles Healy was working in Chiapas on a three-year expedition under the supervision of the Carnegie Institution and funding from the United Fruit Company. During that time he was making a documentary on Central America for the United Fruit Company and exploring new areas that had recently opened up.[97] This included the famous murals of Bonampak, one of the most important archaeological finds of the twentieth century.[98] The murals are one of the finest examples of painting in Mesoamerica and revealed much about Maya culture, including unquestionable evidence of warfare and torture, dramatically going against the prevailing notion of the time that the Maya were a peaceful theocracy.[99]

Unfortunately, archaeologists' interest in ancient sites has had an unwitting consequence, as the chicleros learned that they might contain valuable artifacts and often looted them.[100] In Guatemala, former chicleros have commonly made a living by removing monuments and artifacts to smuggle them abroad.[101] In some cases chicleros have been hired by agents of art dealers to contact them when they find new sites. Although a bilateral treaty was enacted to prohibit the importation of pre-Columbian artifacts into the United States, objects still end up on the art market, and the European art market is bustling.[102] In the late 1990s, George Stuart of the National Geographic Society estimated that over one thousand pieces of high quality polychrome ceramics are stolen out of the Maya area in any given month. The looters usually earn somewhere between $200 and $500 for each vessel, while auction houses and galleries are turning around and selling them to collectors for over $100,000 apiece, resulting in approximately $1.2 billion of cultural patrimony being sold each year.[103]

Looting destroys the material record of past cultures, and, despite the argument that collecting propagates interest and financial support for museums and researchers, it causes indelible damage to the archaeological record. When objects are removed from their original context, they lose virtually all of their meaning, because an object's original use is unknown. Additionally, nearly every archaeologist working in Mesoamerica has come across a looter's trench in a structure that is threatening to collapse because of it. Fortunately, many indigenous peoples have realized that this is not a sustainable source of income and value the importance of preserving their patrimony. In Peru, which has been ravaged by looting since the 1950s, indigenous peoples have developed patrols that watch for looters at archaeological sites and report them to the local authorities.[104] There are even a few cases in which chicleros are working to *conserve* archaeological resources. Archaeologist Richard Hansen hires twenty-seven former chicleros a year as park guards to protect archaeological sites in Guatemala. Regrettably, they are in the minority and are working against a large enterprise that is more interested in making money than preserving cultural patrimony. Carlos Catalán, a chiclero who had become a staunch opponent of looting in Petén, was assassinated in his town of Carmelita. Although he worked to explain that this unsustainable source of income was causing irreparable damage to their cultural heritage, he was killed by a former chiclero turned looter who is serving time in prison for the murder. Apparently Catalán's efforts were a threat to the multimillion dollar looting enterprise that has developed there.[105]

Discussion

Despite the chicleros' general reputation over the last century as violent, promiscuous criminals, there is little that consistently characterizes this often contradictory group. Some are locals who live with their families in the camps, while most come alone from elsewhere and may have few ties to a community. Some are honest and hardworking, while others may be hiding from the law or may engage in regular violence, including murder. Most have an excellent working knowledge of the forest and its resources, although many exhibit beliefs in forest spirits and attribute mythical powers to jungle animals. Although oft reputed to be drunkards, they work long and tedious days under arduous conditions and for little money, and suffer regularly from diseases and injury. Although they have guided archaeologists to some of the most important archaeological finds of the last century, they are more often remembered for robbing those same sites of their artifacts.

This complex and misunderstood group has played a significant role in a truly American industry. For much of the twentieth century these men wandering the forests provided the key ingredient for a product that millions of people enjoyed worldwide. An era of synthetic gums ushered in the near death of their profession, and there are only a handful of men that still make a living by passing their days in the jungle collecting chicle latex. Even fewer sons will learn about the plants and animals from their fathers while attempting to scale a sapodilla. The generational changes in this boom-and-bust lifestyle reflect a pattern that has occurred with numerous extractive economies, including today's tourism industry in the Maya region. Despite the hardships of their profession over the last 125 years, these chicleros have also experienced a kind of freedom that most workers have never known. As one chiclero stated about his life in the forest: "I love being out here! Because here I am free. You know how important that is for me?"[106]

NOTES

Chapter 1. The Birth of the Chewing Gum Tree

1. Quote excerpted from Dibble and Anderson 1961:56. Used with permission of the University of Utah Press.

2. Quote excerpted from *Charlie and the Chocolate Factory* (Dahl 2004[1964]:99). Used with permission of Random House Publishers.

3. For more on the topic of bark tar and the earliest gum chewing, see chapter 3.

4. Simpson and Ogorzaly 2001:372–374.

5. Chadha 1992:1; Orellana 1987:216.

6. Alcorn 2002:51; Smith 1940:301.

7. Higbee 1948:461; Lundell 1933a:15.

8. See Langenheim 2003:50 and Triplett 1999:6, 17 for a discussion of latexes. For more information on the protective character of latex to the sapodilla tree, see chapter 2.

9. In the most general sense, resins are sticky saps that ooze from trees and plants and harden when exposed to air. Natural resins are viscous and often contain volatile oils that, when burned, may release a strong scent through the rising smoke. Today, terpenes, an ingredient of some resins, are used in numerous hygiene products such as soaps and detergents, shampoo, toothpaste, cosmetics, perfumes, and air fresheners because of their distinctive scents and solvent qualities. See discussion in Langenheim 2003:30, 34 and Triplett 1999:6–7.

10. Simpson and Ogorzaly 2001:371. See chapter 4 for more details on the extraction process.

11. Hodge 1955:74–80; Standley 1930.

12. Alcorn 1994:18; Hodge 1955:80.

13. Dibble and Anderson 1961:88. In geology, "bitumen" is a term used for a type of coal-carbon left over from partially decayed plants and is a solid rock that is soft and crumbly, but not really chewable. In this case bitumen is likely the product of natural petroleum that seeps from offshore, which is the product of decayed microscopic organisms. When it reaches the surface, the more volatile materials evaporate, leaving behind a gummy residue that is a kind of tar or asphalt (Diane Smith, personal communication, 2007).

14. McCafferty and McCafferty 1991:26, 32.

15. Dibble and Anderson 1961:90.

16. Balser 1962:376.

17. Dibble and Anderson 1961:89.

18. Dibble and Anderson 1961:89–90.

19. Dibble and Anderson 1961:56.

20. Dibble and Anderson 1961:56, 89.

21. Although McCafferty and McCafferty (1991:26, 32) are referencing bitumen as "chicle," I believe that the idea of gender associations applies to all chicle.

22. Referenced in Dibble and Anderson 1961:77. Frances Berdan notes that she is unsure why Anderson and Dibble translate *tlaaxnelolli* as bitumen-mixed chicle, as bitumen is *chapopotli* (personal communication, 2006).

23. Coggins and Ladd 1992:354–356; Tarkanian and Hosler 1999:120.

24. Tozzer 1966:197 n. 338.

25. Balser 1962:378; Lothrop 1937:147.

26. For a discussion on the charcoal remains at various sites, see Caldwell 1980:261 for Colha; McKillop 1994:133 for Tikal; Hammond et al. 1986:10 and Miksicek et al. 1981:917 for Cuello; Lentz 1990:9 and McKillop 1994:133 for Wild Cane Caye, Pulltrouser Swamp, and Albion Island.

27. For more information on the images of ancestors on Hanab-Pakal's sarcophagus, see Schele and Mathews 1998:119–122. Reference to the Tortuguero Box as zapote wood is found in Coe 1974:51.

28. For more information on the lintels at Chichén Itzá, see Hodge 1955:77, Lundell 1933a:17, and Puleston 1982; on Tikal, see Coe et al. 1961:42–43, 48; and on El Zotz, see Schuster 1999. Tozzer (1966:197 n. 1065) also notes that de Landa indicates that there was a durable wood used as lintels at the site of Izamal in Yucatán State. Although this is usually sapodilla wood, he indicates that in this case de Landa may have meant a tree called *chimtok*, or *Krugiodendron ferreum* (Vahl) Urban. He says that Ralph Roys gave this tree the nickname of "axe-master" because the steel of the axe became brittle when chopping the wood.

29. Crabtree 1968:449–450.

30. Anon. 1900:27.

31. Higbee 1948:461. Today, Maya farmers leave sapodilla trees found in their cornfields untouched when burning the vegetation to clear the land for slash-and-burn agriculture (personal observation of the author).

32. Elite architecture at Cobá often incorporated corbelled arches, which are stepped vaults that result in tall and narrow rooms. See Folan et al. 1979.

33. Folan et al. 1979:699–700.

34. Alcorn 2002:50. For more details on the significance of bats to the sapodilla, see chapter 2. Another argument has been presented for the high distribution of ramón trees (another ancient Maya food tree) currently found on top of ancient ruins: namely, that

after abandonment, tall ruins would provide an ideal growth area for trees such as the ramón and that they are not the remnants of ancient cultivation but rather the result of natural selection (Lambert and Arnason 1982:298–299).

35. The term "ya" is specifically mentioned in Bishop Diego de Landa's volume on Maya culture (Tozzer 1966:199 n. 1083). Thank you to an anonymous reviewer for pointing out that "tzapotl" referenced soft fruits and not just the sapote. For more detailed information on the fruit, see chapter 2.

36. Tozzer 1966:199 n. 1083. Tozzer notes in the footnote of the translation that this is the sapodilla tree. There is similar mention of the fruit in the two-volume *Relaciones Histórico-Geográphicas de la Gobernación de Yucatán*, which was in answer to a survey that the Spanish crown sent out in 1587 inquiring about the products and people of New Spain (see de la Garza et al. 1983:75). Although we do not know who the author was, it is probably the work of the bilingual Maya aristocrat Gaspar Antonio Chi (anonymous reviewer, personal communication, 2007).

37. De la Garza et al. 1983:75.

38. Coe and Coe 1996:61; Tozzer 1966:95 n. 417.

39. Dibble and Anderson 1963:116–117.

40. Coe and Coe 1996:93; see also Hernández 1959:305.

41. Hodder 1985:14.

42. Hastorf 1991; Morehart et al. 2005:257.

43. Coggins and Ladd 1992:350; Stross 1996:178.

44. Coggins and Ladd 1992:345–347.

45. Stross 1996:183–184.

46. Dibble and Anderson 1961:140.

47. Stross 1996:177–178.

48. Stone 2002:23.

49. Ballgame balls (Dávila and Brady 2004:40–41; Triplett 1999:80); figurines (Berdan and Anawalt 1992:114); tips of drumsticks (Stone 2002:22; Tozzer 1966:93 n. 404).

50. Stone 2002:22; Torquemada 1977:430.

51. Stone 2002:21.

52. Curing hoarseness (Dibble and Anderson 1961:145; Stone 2002:22); colic, urinary, and fertility problems, "spitting of blood" (Dibble and Anderson 1961:155; Stone 2002:22; Tarkanian and Hosler 1999:121); ulcers in the ear and lip sores (Dibble and Anderson 1961:141, 145, 146); hemorrhoids and dysentery (Roys 1931:254); headaches and toothaches (Stone 2002:22).

53. Coggins and Ladd 1992:350.

54. Stross 1996:178.

55. Balser 1962:376; Coggins and Ladd 1992:351; Tozzer 1966:197.

Chapter 2. The Botany of the Sapodilla Tree

1. Author's note: When citing a Latin name the first time (for example, *Manilkara zapota* (L.) P. Royen), the author or taxonomic expert who assigned the name is included. This is especially important when discussing the sapodilla tree, as there are many synonyms for the species.

2. For more information on the adulteration of chicle latex, see chapter 3.

3. Plumier 1703:43, pl. 4.

4. Plumier (1703) distinguished two forms of sapota: *Sapota fructu turbinata, minori* and *Sapota fructu ovato, majori*. Their written descriptions separate them on the basis of the fruit shape (the former is turbinate, while the latter is ovate), size, and slight variations in leaf shape.

5. Moore and Stearn 1967:388.

6. Moore and Stearn 1967:386.

7. In addition to the specific taxonomic revisions discussed here, a number of other taxonomists have variously split *M. zapota*, including Cook 1913; Cronquist 1945; Fosberg 1964; Gilly 1943; and Lundell 1968, 1977, 1978.

8. Due to the large number of taxa in certain plant families in the Neotropics, some floras are published in separate volumes. This volume (Pennington 1990) covers the taxonomy of the family Sapotaceae.

9. As the Linnaean system is primarily based upon floral structure, when Pennington (1990) states that it is nondiagnostic, he means that the variation others have used to separate out species is invalid.

10. Some of the more common synonyms seen in the botanical, agricultural and archaeological literature include *Achras zapota* L., *Manilkara achras* (Miller) Fosb., *Manilkara zapotilla* (Jacq.) Gilly, and *Sapota achras* P. Mill. (Moore and Stearn 1967:386).

11. Gillian P. Schultz compiled a list of the most common names that showed up in the literature. This includes aramasi, chiku (India), buah chiku (Malaysia), chicle (Mexico), chico (Philippines, Guatemala, Mexico), chicozapote (Guatemala, Mexico, Venezuela), muy (Guatemala), nispero (Puerto Rico, Central America, Venezuela), sapodilla (Belize, Hispaniola, Dominica), ya (Guatemala, Yucatán Peninsula), zapote, zapote blanco (Mexico, Guatemala, Belize), zapote colorado (Campeche State in Mexico), and zapote morado (Belize).

12. Pennington 1990:61, 63.

13. Pennington 1990:70.

14. Pérez-Arbelaez 1956. Schwartz (1990:141) also notes that while chicle has been tapped in Panama, Honduras, Colombia, and Venezuela, the primary areas of growth and exportation have always been Quintana Roo, Mexico, the Petén in Guatemala, and northern Belize.

15. Espejel 1987; Heaton et al. 1999:627; personal observation by Gillian P. Schultz. Please note, there is no common name for *Terminalia amazonia*.

16. Sympodial branching is in contrast to monopodial branching, in which the trunk or stem has one main axis with small lateral branches. Monopodial branching is particularly attractive for horticulture and creates a lush and broad canopy.

17. Karling 1942a:49; Morton 1987:397.

18. Flowering and fruiting phenology is based on label data from the Tropicos database of the Missouri Botanical Garden 2006 and the Virtual Herbarium at the New York Botanical Garden 2006.

19. Simpson and Ogorzaly 2001:375.

20. Morton 1987:393; Mickelbart 1996:442.

21. Morton 1987:395; Kute and Shete 1995:478; Mickelbart 1996:440.

22. Mickelbart and Marler 1996; Singh et al. 1997.

23. Mickelbart 1996:440.

24. Morton 1987:395; Singh et al. 1997:265–266.

25. Morton 1987:395; Pennington 1990:66.

26. Piatos and Knight 1975:464–465.

27. Previously, scholars had not observed insects pollinating cultivated sapodilla flowers, and thus they believed that the wind was the primary source for moving pollen from one flower to the next (Patil and Narwadkar 1974; Farooqi and Rao 1976). For more information on insect pollination, see Reddi 1989:409.

28. Reddi 1989:409.

29. See Mickelbart 1996 for a review.

30. Alcorn 2002:50. Bartlett (1935) and Lundell (1937) have also commented on this. See further discussion of the Folan et al. 1979 study on the ancient Maya impact on sapodilla tree distribution in chapter 1.

31. Chin and Roberts 1980; Farnsworth 2000.

32. Cruz-Rodríguez and López Mata 2004.

33. Heithaus et al. 1975; Fleming 1988:322–323.

34. Pennington 1990:10; Fægri and Van der Pijl 1971:154.

35. The distances traveled by bats are based on calculations from recapture data in the course of one season (Montiel et al. 2006)

36. Alcorn 2002:50–51; Heithaus et al. 1975:847; Montiel et al. 2006:273. Because animals are known to congregate in sapodilla trees for the fruit, hunters often stake out these trees (anonymous reviewer, personal communication, 2007).

37. Heithaus et al. 1975:843, 844; Greenhall 1957:409–410.

38. Barbour 1945:210–211.

39. Montiel et al. 2006:274.

40. Alcorn 2002:50. However, humans have certainly been solely responsible for the species' distribution outside of its natural range.

41. Alcorn 2002:50; O'Farrill et al. 2006.

42. Klimstra and Dooley 1990:268.

43. A hectare (ha) is the equivalent of 2.471 acres. Dbh (diameter at breast height) is a standard measure of tree stems taken at 1.37 m (4.5 ft) above the forest floor. It is used by botanists, ecologists, and foresters to determine growth, volume, yield, and forest potential for harvest.

44. See Gentry 1995 and Dewalt and Chave 2004 for two recent reviews of tropical forest structure.

45. Flynn et al. 2006.

46. Recalcitrance is a common trait in tropical trees, particularly those found in wetter habitats. See Farnsworth 2000:125.

47. Tweddle et al. 2003:296.

48. Cruz Rodríguez and López Mata 2004:230.

49. Alcorn 2002:51.

50. The U.S. Department of Commerce ranked Hurricane Dean, which hit the Yucatán Peninsula in 2007, as the ninth most intense Atlantic hurricane.

51. Whigham et al. 1998:268–272.

52. Morton 1987:393.

53. Alcorn 2002:51.

54. In the Philippines, some common cultivars are Ponderosa, Rangel, Native, Formosa, and Sao Manila. See Morton 1987:393.

55. Cultivars in these locations are less studied than those in India and the Philippines. See Morton 1987; Mickelbart 1996; Vélez et al. 1989; SOFRI 2002.

56. Successful cultivars in Florida include Prolific, Brown Sugar, Modello, Russel, and Tikal (Morton 1987:394; Kute and Shete 1995; Mickelbart 1996:444; Balerdi et al. 2005).

57. Morton 1987:393; Mickelbart 1996:439.

58. Common cultivars in India include Kalipatti, Cricket Ball, Oval, Oblong, Badam, Calcutta Round, Bangalore, Baramasi, Bhuri, Dwarapudi, Gouranga, Guthi, Kirtibarti, Pilipatti, Singapore, and Round (Morton 1987:393–394; Chadha 1992:6; Kute and Shete 1995:476; Chundawat and Bhuva 1982:154; Balerdi et al. 2005).

59. Kute and Shete 1995:476; Mickelbart 1996:443.

60. Kute and Shete 1995:476; Campbell et al. 1987:282. Even though the sapodilla is considered an invasive species in Florida, horticulturists have grown many plants in the United States for their physical appearance rather than productive value.

61. Gandhi 1956:9; Mickelbart 1996:441; Heaton 1997:13.

62. Gandhi 1956:9; Kute and Shete 1995:478.

63. Madhava-Rao et al. 1975:7; Mickelbart 1996:440.

64. Rootstocks of several related species have been found to be particularly useful for this purpose, including *Manilkara hexandra* (Roxb.) Dubard and *M. emarginata* (Bakar) Lam. and Meeuse. See Chandler 1958:330–332; Ogden and Campbell 1980. Other species used as rootstocks include *Madhuca indica* J. F. Gmel. and *Bassia longifolia* L., as well as seedlings of *M. zapota* itself. See Gandhi 1956:18; Ogden and Campbell 1980:90; Kute and Shete 1995:478.

65. Of these techniques, veneer grafting, also known as bark grafting, has the highest rate of success. In veneer grafting, the scion is cut and inserted just under the bark of the rootstock so that the vascular tissue of the two are joined together (this is analogous to the connection of blood vessels in organ transplants). See Hussain and Bukhari 1977:54–55.

66. Plantations are located primarily in the Maharastra, Gujarat, Andhra Pradesh, Madras, and Bengal states in India. See Chadha 1992:2.

67. Chadha 1992:8.

68. Growth hormones include alpha naphthalene acetic acid (NAA) and 3–indolebu-tyric acid (IBA). See Gandhi 1956:14; Chadha 1992:8.

69. Purohit and Singhvi 1998:220.

70. Most plant cells remain unspecialized as adults, so if a plant is damaged and the remaining cells receive the correct stimulus, they can grow into a whole new plant. This occurs naturally with no assistance in many plants, which is why cuttings of some house plants stuck in water will produce new roots. This is also why we battle with weeds—unless every single bit of them is removed from the soil, they can grow into a whole new plant.

71. Purohit and Singhvi 1998:226.

72. Morton 1987:396; Chadha 1992:11; Mickelbart 1996:441; Balerdi et al. 2005:5.

73. Avilan et al. 1980:14; Bafna et al. 1983:67; Laborem et al. 1981:35. During the first ten years or so, sapodilla are often grown in the same field with other, smaller tree-fruit species such as papaya and pomegranate, in the same way that apple farmers raise cover or annual crops beside their immature trees before they begin to bear fruit. The effects of this kind of multi-use farming upon sapodilla production have not been investigated (Kute and Shete 1995:479; Chadha 1992:11).

74. Gandhi 1956:34. Researchers have also conducted extensive investigations into the insect pests of sapodilla and their control in India, Puerto Rico, Florida, and Venezuela, while a few smaller studies have examined pests in Vietnam and in its native range (Butani 1975; Medina-Gaud et al. 1987; Peters et al. 1984; Rubio-Espina 1968; Van Mele and Cuc Nguyen 2001). In India, a total of twenty-five insect species have been reported to cause damage to sapodilla, but two are of particular importance: the chiku moth (*Nephopteryx eugraphella* Ragonot) and the chiku bud borer (*Anarsia achrasella*) (Chadha 1992:12). The larval forms of both of these species are responsible for most of the damage, with the

former attacking the leaves, flowers, and young fruits, while the latter primarily damages the flower buds. Other harmful insects found in India include the leaf miner (*Acrocercops gemoniella*), scolytid beetles (*Hypothenemus birmanus*), and fruit flies (*Dacus correctus*) (Butani 1975; Chadha 1992:12; Gandhi 1956:34–35; Peters et al. 1984). In the New World, fruit flies of the genus *Anastrepha* are reported to be problematic—particularly the Caribbean fruit fly (*Anastrepha suspensa*) and the sapota fruit fly (*A. serpentina*) (Balerdi et al. 2005:5; Medina-Gaud et al. 1987:130; Rubio-Espina 1968:2). Both of these flies deposit their eggs in the developing fruit, allowing the larvae to consume it upon hatching. In Florida, the bloom moth (*Banisia myrsusalis*) attacks the flowers and prevents pollination (Balerdi et al. 2005:5). Only one study has examined the insects associated with sapodilla in its native range and found that the larvae of the sapodilla bud borer (*Zamagiria dixolophella*) are problematic in Chiapas, Mexico (Iruegas et al. 2002).

75. In India, the leaves are attacked by leaf spot disease (*Phaeophleospora indica*), which causes the leaves to prematurely drop and reduces the trees' capacity for photosynthesis and overall productivity (Chadha 1992:12). From the commercial production perspective, the diseases that attack the fruit post-harvest appear to be the biggest problem. The fruit's high moisture content makes it prone to a number of fungal and microbial pathogens, including soft rot (*Phomopsis sapotae*), sour rot (*Geotrichum candidum*), Cladosporium rot (*Cladosporium oxysporum*), blue mold rot (*Penicillium italicum*), and fruit rot (*Phytophthora palmivora*) (Balerdi et al. 2005:4; Chadha 1992:14; Khare et al. 1994:323; Mickelbart 1996:444).

76. González and Feliciano 1953; Mulla and Desle 1990:267; and Relekar et al. 1991:105.

77. Mulla and Desle 1990:267.

78. Relekar et al. 1991:105.

79. Lakshminarayana and Subramanyam 1966:153.

80. Abdul Karim et al. 1987; Gandhi 1956:33; Lakshminarayana 1980:417.

81. Lakshminarayana 1980:416.

82. Lakshminarayana 1980:417; Mickelbart 1996:444.

83. Broughton and Wong 1979; de Morais et al. 2006; Lakshminarayana 1980:417.

84. Chadha 1992:14; Jain and Jain 1998:328; Lakshminarayana 1980:418.

85. Chadha 1992:14; Lakshminarayana 1980:418.

86. Kashanipour and McGee 2004:55, 64.

87. Ankli et al. 2002; Mutchnick and McCarthy 1997:166; de Los Angeles et al. 2003:2465.

88. Morton 1987:198. For more information about the ancient use of latex as tooth fillings, see chapter 1.

89. Lans et al. 2000:208.

90. Morton 1987:198.

91. Einbond et al. 2004; Hart et al. 1973; Ma et al. 2003; Sandermann and Funke 1970:413; Shui et al. 2004.

92. Saponins belong to a class of molecules known as glycosides that yield a sugar (glycone) such as glucose or arabinose and one or more nonsugar substances (aglycones) when they are hydrolyzed, or broken down. Saponins specifically yield one of four simple sugars and a nonsugar substance, sapogenin, which are characterized as either steroids or triterpenes. See Agarwal and Rastogi 1974; Sandermann and Funke 1970:413.

93. Sandermann and Funke 1970. For more information on the sapodilla wood carvings at archaeological sites, see chapter 1.

94. Waller 2000:1.

95. Tannins, which produce the tartness in fruits, get their name from their application in the tanning or curing of animal skins, which humans have carried out for several thousand years. See Simpson and Ogorzaly 2001:375.

96. Einbond et al. 2004; Hart et al. 1973; Ma et al. 2003; Shui et al. 2004; Sandermann and Funke 1970:413.

97. Simpson and Ogorzaly 2001:375.

98. Shui et al. 2004:7838.

99. Ma et al. 2003:984–985.

Chapter 3. The History of the Chewing Gum Industry in the Americas

1. The quote from Will Rogers was originally published in a 1923 *Washington Post* column (Rogers 1923:80). Will Rogers™ is a trademark of the Rogers Company, licensed by CMG Worldwide, Inc., www.CMGWorldwideInc.com

2. The quote from Elbert Hubbard is excerpted from the book *Preachments: Elbert Hubbard's Selected Writings, Part 4* (Hubbard 1998:467). Although we do not know exactly how much gum U.S. citizens were consuming at the turn of the century, in the year 1920 the two major gum manufacturers of the day (Wrigley's and Adams Gum) were turning out over 45 million sticks of gum per day (Adams: Anon. 1920b:9, Wrigley: Feld 1925:XX5; Hendrickson 1976:93–94) or approximately 112.5 billion sticks annually (assuming fifty weeks of production, five days a week × 45 million sticks a day). In the same year, there were approximately six thousand book titles published a year with fewer than 150 million copies in circulation. The 1927 U.S. Census demonstrated that the average person bought two books a year, but as a whole Americans spent more than $3 billion on "luxuries," which included everything from "chewing gum to fireworks to jewelry—a figure fully twenty times greater than the amount spent on books" (Benton 1997:273–274).

3. See chapter 1 for more information on pre-Columbian use of chicle by the Maya and Aztec.

4. Ötzi the Ice Man is a 5,300-year-old body that was found on the Italian/Austrian border and is the oldest and best-preserved mummy ever recovered. Archaeologists found clothing, plant materials, a quiver with arrows, and a copper axe associated with the body. The copper axe was attached to a handle and was attached with bitumen and sinew. For more information, see Dickson et al. 2005.

5. Aveling and Heron 1999:579, 583.

6. Pliny 1968:37, 53, 267.

7. Edmonds and Clark 1989:64.

8. Mabberley 1997:555.

9. Gustaitis 1998; Hendrickson 1976:31–32.

10. Schwartz 1990:139–140.

11. Elden 1926:XX5.

12. Landon 1935:184.

13. See, for example, Gustaitis 1998; Hendrickson 1976:46–47; Konrad 1995:97, 1987:466–467; Landon 1935:183–184; Redclift 2003:162, 2004:18; Scheina 2002:83; and Stanford 1934:199–200.

14. Hanighen 1934; Scheina 2002.

15. Konrad 1995:97.

16. These tales are referenced in Hendrickson 1976:47.

17. Miguel Sandoval, personal communication, 2006.

18. Information obtained from U.S. Bureau of the Census 1880; U.S. Bureau of the Census 1920; Anon. 1905b:2–4.

19. Hendrickson 1976:46.

20. Anon. 1956:17; Scheina 2002:83.

21. Anon. 1884:8, 1928b:6; Gustaitis 1998; Hanighen 1934:298; Hendrickson 1976:46–47; Konrad 1995:97; Landon 1935:183–184; Redclift 2003:162, 2004:18–24; Scheina 2002:83; and Stanford 1934:199–200.

22. Hanighen 1934:7; Scheina 2002:5–6.

23. Hanighen 1934:15; Scheina 2002:8.

24. Hanighen 1934:50, 69; Scheina 2002:18, 24.

25. Hanighen 1934:120; Scheina 2002:28.

26. Hanighen 1934:112–115; Scheina 2002:32–33.

27. Hanighen 1934:126; Scheina 2002:33.

28. Hanighen 1934:127; Scheina 2002:34–35.

29. The Pastry War of 1833 occurred because roughly five years earlier some Mexican soldiers had caused about 800 pesos of damage to a French-owned bakery outside of Mexico City. In an attempt to recoup their losses, the French government added these damages to other existing debt, threw in interest, and announced that the Mexican

government owed them 60,000 pesos. To intimidate them into paying, France sent a navy squadron to the Gulf Coast of Mexico. However, their poorly supplied ships and yellow-fever infected soldiers failed to coerce the Mexicans. France then added 200,000 pesos to the debt to cover the cost of the expedition and threatened to attack the coast of Veracruz. A battle ensued and Mexico declared war on France. Santa Anna led a raid against the French and was hit in the left leg and hand by cannon shot. This injury stopped Santa Anna's raid and caused the French to withdraw. Hanighen 1934:143–155; Scheina 2002:36–40.

30. Scheina 2002:77.

31. Hanighen 1934:283.

32. Anon. 1884:8.

33. Nadal 1999:23–24.

34. Hendrickson 1976:48–49.

35. Hanighen 1934:306; Scheina 2002:85.

36. Anon. 1884:8.

37. Hendrickson 1976:49–50.

38. Anon. 1956:17; Scheina 2002:83.

39. Anon. 1884:8.

40. Anon. 1956:17; Landon 1935:184; Simpson and Ogorzaly 2001:371.

41. Anon. 1956:17; Barrera de Jorgenson 1993:15; Karling 1942a:38; Landon 1935:184; Simpson and Ogorzaly 2001:371; Stanford 1934:200.

42. Schwartz 1990:140.

43. Anon. 1890:112.

44. Landon 1935:184.

45. Hendrickson 1976:53.

46. Wald 1979:A1.

47. Anon. 1916:18.

48. Morrone 2001:358–360.

49. David Kenny, personal communication, 2006.

50. Lanigan-Schmidt 2003:154.

51. Morrone 2001:360.

52. Anon. 1919:11.

53. Anon. 1920a:6.

54. Anon. 1920b:9.

55. Hendrickson 1976:87.

56. Feld 1925:XX5; Hendrickson 1976:88.

57. Feld 1925:XX5; Hendrickson 1976:89; King 1971:F1.

58. Collins 1927:34; Feld 1925:XX5; Hendrickson 1976:90–91.

59. Anon. 1932a:4.

60. Feld 1925:XX5; Hendrickson 1976:93–94.

61. Collins 1929:13; King 1971:F1.

62. Overwork (Anon. 1923a); Ku Klux Klan accusations (Anon. 1923b:14, 1923c:16).

63. Tower 1976:92. British Honduras was a colony of the United Kingdom until 1973, when the name was officially changed to Belize.

64. Anon. 1932a:4.

65. Anon. 1893:8.

66. Anon. 1907:6; Hendrickson 1976:75.

67. Anon. 1906:6; Anon. 1907:6; Hendrickson 1976:75.

68. Hendrickson 1976:75; Schwartz 1990:140.

69. Hendrickson 1976:77, 79.

70. Anon. 1892b:1; Anon. 1893:8.

71. Anon. 1906:6; Hendrickson 1976:79.

72. Morrow 1908:E1.

73. Anon. 1937a:19.

74. Hendrickson 1976:83.

75. Landon 1935:184, 190.

76. Goodnough 1998:B7.

77. Anon. 1930:18.

78. Anon. 1946:22.

79. Hendrickson 1976:84–85.

80. Anon. 1946:22.

81. Mohawk Valley Library System 1999. The American Chicle Company also used attractive young women known as "sampling girls" to hawk their wares. They worked in teams of four to eight, dressed in orange satin outfits, and passed out five thousand sticks of gum a day (Hendrickson 1976:104–105).

82. Anon. 1901:WF5; Anon. 1899:3; Landon 1935:184.

83. Anon. 1906:6.

84. Anon. 1901:WF5.

85. Anon. 1928a:19.

86. Hendrickson 1976:80.

87. Anon. 1892a:9.

88. Alcorn 1994:19.

89. Landon 1935:185. See also Vadillo López 2001.

90. Anon. 1904:14.

91. Martín del Campo 1999:46.

92. Forero and Redclift 2006:70; Konrad 1995:97, 102.

93. Barrera de Jorgenson 1993:10–11; Patch 1993; Reed 1964; Rugeley 1996, 2001; Sullivan 1989.

94. Edwards 1986:124.

95. Sullivan 1989:36.

96. Barrera de Jorgensen 1993:18.

97. Schwartz 1990:139.

98. Karling 1942b:78; Landon 1935:186; Schwartz 1990:141.

99. Barrera de Jorgenson 1993:11; Konrad 1995:98; Martín del Campo 1999:46.

100. Schwartz 1990:156.

101. Barrera de Jorgenson 1993:16.

102. Villa R. 1945:63.

103. Konrad 1995:98.

104. Mathews and Lizama-Rogers 2005.

105. Karling 1942a:38–39; Konrad 1995:98; see also Alcorn 1994:24.

106. Schwartz 1990:155–156, 1974:377.

107. A later study by Professor Hollingworth (1939) of Columbia University demonstrated that chewing did in fact reduce muscular tension and calmed nerves.

108. Hoar 1924:1.

109. Nichols 1930:X12.

110. Elden 1926:XX5.

111. Nichols 1930:X12; Landon 1935:183.

112. Forero and Redclift 2006:69.

113. Redclift 2004:69–71.

114. Anon. 1929:20.

115. Forero and Redclift 2006:72–73; Redclift 2004:70–73.

116. Schwartz 1990:148. Konrad (1991:146–147) argues that over 29 percent of Belizean forest exports (wood, chicle, rubber, etc.) came from outside of the country.

117. Anon. 1926:17; Anon. 1929:20.

118. Anon. 1929:20.

119. Reed 1964:254.

120. Redclift 2004.

121. Anon. 1935:A13; Karling 1935:580.

122. Alcorn 1994:22; Lundell 1933a:20.

123. Karling 1935:582–583.

124. Karling 1942c:554.

125. Higbee 1948:462.

126. Redclift 2004.

127. Hodge 1955:80.

128. Landon 1935:186. Hodge (1955:76) also later reported that cultivated sapodilla trees have significantly less latex than those found naturally in the forests.

129. Jelutong, gutta siak (Nichols 1930:X12); wild fig (Hodge 1955:80).

130. Anon. 1947a:34. Schwartz (1990:153) estimates that between the years 1900 and 1950 more than half of the residents of the Petén district in Guatemala were dependent on the chicle industry.

131. Schwartz 1990:140.

132. Redclift 2004; Torres 2003:72.

133. Anon. 1924:26.

134. Nichols 1930:X12.

135. Landon 1935:188.

136. Nichols 1930:X12.

137. Topps History 2004.

138. Anon. 1942a:31; Anon. 1942b:10.

139. Anon. 1942b:10.

140. Anon. 1944b:14.

141. Anon. 1945:M8. That same year (1944), Philip Wrigley announced that he would resign due to differences of opinion with the board of directors. Privately it was suggested that his resignation was a result of members of the board disagreeing with Wrigley's assessment that the war would last much longer than they thought and his restriction of manufacturing gum. Publicly, they attributed his resignation to his being too much of a micromanager, including writing and approving all advertising copy, and being physically worn down and with little enthusiasm left for his job (Anon. 1944a:26).

142. Simms 2003:E1.

143. Neumeister 2006.

144. Noyes 2006:3.

145. Hendrickson 1976:166.

146. Mitgang 1959:SM75–SM76.

147. Dimeglio 2001; Mitgang 1959:SM75–SM76.

148. Hendrickson 1976:167; Phillips 1964:27.

149. Van Gelder 1975:33.

150. Stamler 2001:C6.

151. Dimeglio 2001.

152. Anon. 1983:D2; Hammonds 1982:155.

153. Hammonds 1982:155.

154. At the suggestion of an anonymous reviewer, Jennifer Mathews compiled the gum-related songs through Internet searches. Uncle Dave Macon's song can be found on the boxed set *Classic Sides: 1924–1938*. Lonnie Donegan's song, originally released in

1956, can be found on the 2006 album *The Skiffle King: Fiftieth Anniversary Edition*. The Policarpo Aguilar song can be found on the rare album *Geografia Musical*. "El Chiclero" by Chalo Campos y Su Orquesta is from the 2006 release *30 Éxitos*. The song "El Chiclet" is found on the 2001 Frenesi de Merengue album *Merengue Superhits*.

155. Thank you to Professor Rosana Blanco-Caño for her assistance in providing the chicle-related phrases (personal communication, 2007).

156. Hendrickson 1976:107.

157. Redclift 2004:13.

158. Post 1956:54.

159. See, for example, Post 1969.

160. Post 2004:25, 171.

161. Hendrickson 1976:106–107.

162. Anon. 1937b.

163. The song was released on the 2006 live album *Serie Immortales: En Concierto*. Thank you to Professor Pablo Martínez for his suggestion of this song.

164. Konrad 1995:98; Barrera de Jorgenson 1993:17.

165. Aldrete 1998:8.

166. Anon. 1952:7.

167. Abandoned railroads (Mathews and Lizama-Rogers 2005); drop in workforce (Konrad 1995:97).

168. Schwartz 1990:140.

169. Barrera de Jorgenson 1993:17; Konrad 1995:98.

170. Hendrickson 1976:198–202; Wardlaw 1997:90–97; Young 1990:15–20.

171. Dougherty 1975:57.

172. Anon. 1960:56.

173. McCormacls 1975:156; Rubinstein 1976:B5.

174. Anon. 1984:A18.

175. Cohn 1980:D8.

176. Fleming-Michael 2006.

177. Sohn 2007:F1.

178. Sohn 2007:F1.

179. Anon. 1939b:12. See also 1939a.

180. Stratton and Schleman 1955:87.

181. Anon. 2002.

182. Anon. 2007.

183. Hollingworth 1939.

184. Edgar 1998:26.

185. Wilkinson et al. 2002.

186. Young 2002.

187. Tucha et al. 2004.

188. Moore 2005:40.

189. Forbes 400 Richest Americans 2007. Note that at the time that this book was going to press, William Buffet and the Mars Corporation was acquiring Wrigley for $23 billion, which would make it the largest candy company in the world (Sorkin 2008; Martin 2008).

190. Barrera de Jorgensen 1993:17; Konrad 1995:98. In 1998, all Guatemalan chicle was slated for purchase by two companies that were exporting to Japan (McNab 1998:27).

191. Martín del Campo 1999:13–15.

192. Aldrete 1998:1–4; see also Plan Piloto 1998.

193. Alcorn 1994:21–22.

194. Deborah Schimberg, personal communication, 2007.

195. Verve Inc. also sponsors scholarships for the sons and daughters of chicleros to attend college. For more information or to make a donation, contact them at (401) 351-6415 or via e-mail at info@gleegum.com (Deborah Schimberg, personal communication, 2007).

196. Hernández 2008.

Chapter 4. The Chicleros

1. Quote from "Stranded on an Unexplored Coast," from *The Lost World of Quintana Roo* by Michel Peissel (1963:102), renewed 1991 by Michel Peissel. Used with permission of Dutton, a division of Penguin Group (USA) Inc.

2. Quote from *Forest Society: A Social History of Petén, Guatemala* by Norman B. Schwartz (1990:147). Used with permission of University of Pennsylvania Press.

3. Schwartz 1990:184.

4. Fox 1961:215, 222.

5. Chardon 1963:177.

6. Everton 1991:168–169.

7. Macías Zapata 1992:135; Reed 1964:235; Deborah Schimberg, personal communication, 2007. In addition to chicle, the Compañia del Cuyo y Anexas extracted cabinet woods, cattle, rubber, salt, sugar, tobacco, and vanilla (Konrad 1991:151).

8. The chicle industry did not expand within the Petén region until the 1920s and 1930s, and even then latex was a distant third in imports behind coffee and bananas (Schwartz 1987:166; 1990:138).

9. Alcorn 1994:40–42.

10. Egler 1947:207.

11. Fox 1961:224.

12. Kim 1971:14–20; Patterson 2000:4.

13. Reed 1964:235; see also Barrera de Jorgenson 1993:12; Karling 1942a:39; Konrad 1995:99.

14. Schwartz 1990:152–153.

15. Schwartz 1990:156; see also Schwartz 1972:371.

16. Konrad 1995:97; Schwartz 1990:152–153.

17. Amram Jr. 1948:125.

18. Karling 1942a:39.

19. Schwartz 1990:177.

20. Karling 1942a:39.

21. Alcorn 1994:24.

22. Dugelby 1995:68.

23. Konrad 1995:99; Schwartz states camps in Petén had 10–25 workers, plus a cook (1972:380).

24. Beteta 1937:35–36.

25. McNab 1998:26, 29–30, 72–74. See also Forero and Redclift 2006:68–69.

26. This folk knowledge was confirmed by scientific studies conducted in the 1930s, which found that the greatest yield of latex occurred at 6:00 a.m. and on humid days. After the sun rose, the latex thickened, and in some cases stopped flowing (Karling 1934:161, 169).

27. This same study found that during the dry season the actual diameter of the sapodilla tree trunks shrunk, due to lack of moisture, which would explain why the rainy season was preferred for collecting. See Karling 1934:177–178, 188.

28. Everton 1991:98.

29. Schwartz 1990:142–143.

30. Florentino Chacón, personal communication, 2002. See also Alcorn 1994:22–23; Egler 1947:194–195; Everton 1991:98; Heyder 1930:108–111; Hodge 1955, 79–80; Karling 1942a:39–47; Konrad 1995:100; Lundell 1933a:18–20; Mathews and Lizama-Rogers 2005; Sullivan 1989:36.

31. Karling 1934:171, 189–190.

32. Florentino Chacón, personal communication, 2002; Alberto Sanchéz, personal communication, 2002; Macduff Everton, personal communication, 2006. See also Alcorn 1994:22–23; Anon. 1953; Heyder 1930:108–111; Hodge 1955, 79–80; Karling 1942a:39–47; Konrad 1995:100–101; Lundell 1933a:18–20; Mathews and Lizama-Rogers 2005; Villa R. 1945:62–63.

33. Lundell 1933a:20.

34. Konrad 1995:101.

35. Konrad 1995:98.

36. Villa R. 1945:63.

37. Alcorn 1994:20–21; Heyder 1930:110–111; Karling 1942c; Peissel 1963:228.

38. Karling 1942b:76–77.

39. Schwartz 1990:163.

40. Escalona Ramos 1940:208–223; Möller 1986. See also Mathews and Lizama-Rogers 2005 for a more thorough discussion of the Puerto Morelos-Santa María rail, and Möller 1986 for additional information on the Chan Santa Cruz-Vigía Chico section.

41. One section of railroad that was roughly fifty miles long reportedly cost the Mexican government $1,500,000 at the turn of the twentieth century (Anon. 1905a:X3).

42. Chardon 1963: figs. 6.7, 6.8, 6.9; Decauville 1993:150; Neale 1992:146–147.

43. Escalona Ramos 1940:216; Mathews and Lizama-Rogers 2005:116–117; Shattuck 1933.

44. Karling 1942a:49; Mathews and Lizama-Rogers 2005:117; Shattuck 1933:163.

45. Everton 1991:93–94.

46. Schwartz 1990:147.

47. Alberto Sánchez, personal communication, 2002; see also Mathews and Lizama-Rogers 2005:116.

48. Schwartz 1990:147.

49. Thompson 1961:173. Some chicleros believed that the ulcer was caused by ticks or fleas rather than the black fly (Ortega Canto et al. 1996:36).

50. Thompson 1961:174.

51. Menéndez 1936:163; Peissel 1963:228; Shattuck 1933:164–166, 321; Thompson 1961:174.

52. Ortega Canto et al. 1996:39.

53. Clarke 1934:108.

54. Konrad 1995:101–102.

55. Everton 1991:99. Some Maya still tell these stories today and often report killing snakes because they have stingers in the tail (Justine Shaw, personal communication, 2006; personal observation of the author).

56. Alberto Sánchez, personal communication, 2002.

57. Snake bites and fevers (Anon. 1931:84; Everton 1991:99); amoebic dysentery (McNab 1998:30; Peissel 1963:228).

58. Lizardi Ramos 1937b:2; McNab 1998:31; Schwartz 1972:379, 1990:176.

59. Anon. 1931:84.

60. Karling 1942a:41; Konrad 1995:100–101.

61. Shattuck 1933:165–166.

62. Anon. 1929.

63. Lundell 1933b:166.

64. Alcorn 1994; Everton 1991:90; Karling 1942a:41; Konrad 1995:98; Schwartz 1990.

65. Atran 1993:677.

66. Karling 1942a:41; Konrad 1995:98.

67. Konrad 1995:101–102; Peissel 1963:96–97.

68. Everton 1991:90; Peissel 1963:34. The Cruzob Maya of Chan Santa Cruz in Quintana Roo had been rebelling since the Caste War of the 1850s and were known for being fierce warriors and protectors of the land. Up to today, few outsiders have been accepted in this region. For more information, see, for example, Everton 1991 and Reed 1964.

69. Anon. 1931:84.

70. Konrad 1995:102; Schwartz 1972:378–379.

71. Peissel 1963:96.

72. Peissel 1963:101.

73. Mathews and Lizama-Rogers 2005:114.

74. Peissel 1963:50–51, 101.

75. Schwartz 1990:175.

76. Gann 1918:37.

77. Shattuck 1933:165, 275.

78. Lizardi Ramos 1937a:2.

79. Schwartz 1990:174–175.

80. Anon. 1931:84; Everton 1991:95–96; Peissel 1963:96.

81. Everton 1991:90, 94.

82. Konrad 1995:98; Barrera de Jorgenson 1993:17. For more information about the crash of the chicle industry after the introduction of synthetic gums, see chapter 3.

83. Everton 1991:109, 118.

84. Deborah Schimberg, personal communication, 2006.

85. An example of this kind of small-scale tourism is found near the defunct chiclero village of Central Vallarta in Quintana Roo and is run by a family of former chicleros (José Montoya, personal communication, 2006). Another chicle "village" can be found at the Dr. Alfredo Barrera Marin Botanical Garden in Puerto Morelos, Quintana Roo.

86. Alcorn 1994:23.

87. Lizardi Ramos 1937a:2.

88. Molina Montes 1978:1.

89. Coe 1999:127.

90. Morley 1943:214.

91. Anon. 1932b:258; Anon. 1932c:24; Anon. 1932d:20; Lundell 1933b.

92. Anon. 1932b:258–259.

93. Coe 2005:102.

94. Lundell 1933b:179.

95. Ruppert and Denison 1943:1–2.

96. Reese-Taylor n.d.

97. Ruppert 1947:177; 1955:9.

98. Anon. 1947b:56.

99. Miller 1986:4.

100. Alcorn 1994:19; Anon. 1947b:56; Peissel 1963:96–97; and personal observation of author.

101. Hansen 1997:48.

102. Anon. 1973:512.

103. Hansen 1997:48.

104. Atwood 2003:44–45.

105. Hansen 1997:48; Richard Hansen, personal communication, 2006.

106. Everton 1991:109.

Bibliography

Abdul-Karim, M. N. B., S. A. Tarmizi, and A. A. Bakar
1987   The Physio-Chemical Changes in Ciku (*Achras sapota* L.) of Jantung Variety. *Pertanika* 10 (3): 277–282.

Agarwal, S. K., and R. P. Rastogi
1974   Triterpenoid Saponins and Their Genins. *Phytochemistry* 13 (12): 2623–2645.

Alcorn, P. W.
1994   The Chicle Tree (*Manilkara zapota*) in Northwest Belize: Natural History, Forest Floristics, and Management. Master's thesis, University of Florida.
2002   Botany and Ecology of Chicle. In *Tapping the Green Market—Management and Certification of Non-Timber Forest Products*, edited by Patricia Shanley, Alan R. Pierce, Sarah A. Laird, and Abraham Guillén, 49–59. London: Earthscan Publications.

Aldrete, Manuel
1998   Desarollo Institución al Chicle/Miel en la Comunidad de Señor, Ejido X-Maben y Anexos en el Municipio de Felipe Carillo Puerto, Quintana Roo. Unpublished manuscript in possession of the author.

Amram, David W., Jr.
1948   Eastern Chiapas Revisited. *Geographical Review* 38 (1): 120–126.

Andrews, Anthony P.
1985   The Archaeology and History of Northern Quintana Roo. In *Geology and Hydrogeology of the Yucatán and Quaternary Geology of Northeastern Yucatán Peninsula*, edited by C. Ward, A. E. Weidie, and W. Back, 127–143. New Orleans: New Orleans Geological Society.

Ankli, A., M. Heinrich, P. Bork, L. Wolfram, P. Bauerfeind, R. Brun, C. Schmid, C. Weiss, R. Bruggisser, J. Gertsch, M. Wasescha, and O. Sticherk
2002   Yucatec Mayan Medicinal Plants: Evaluation Based on Indigenous Uses. *Journal of Ethnopharmacology* 79 (1): 43–52.

Anonymous
1884   Juice of the Sapota Tree. *New York Times*, March 24, p. 8.

1890   *Industries and Wealth of Brooklyn.* New York City: American Publishing and Engraving Company.

1892a   He Makes Chewing Gum. *New York Times,* July 14, p. 9.

1892b   Chewing Gum Wins the Day. *New York Times,* August 10, p. 1.

1893   Major Hayes Astonished. *New York Times,* May 5, p. 8.

1899   The Chewing-Gum Trust. *New York Times,* June 3, p. 3.

1900   Weapons of the Maya Indians. *New York Times,* March 4, p. 27.

1901   American Chicle Expansion. *New York Times,* December 15, p. WF5.

1904   Shortage of Chicle Advances Its Price: Chewing Gum Trade Affected by Rise in Raw Material. *New York Times,* April 3, p. 14.

1905a   Some Fancy Dress Gowns (the Gum America Chews). *New York Times,* July 9, p. X3.

1905b   Chewing Gum Pioneer Died in Brooklyn To-Day. *Brooklyn Daily Eagle,* February 7, pp. 2–4.

1906   Chewing Gum: It Makes a Cleveland Millionaire and a Divorce. *Washington Post,* October 4, p. 6.

1907   A Romance in Chewing Gum. *Washington Post,* May 16, p. 6.

1916   Thomas Adams' Home in Bay Shore. *Brooklyn Daily Eagle,* May 31, p. 18.

1919 $2,000,000 Factory for Chewing Gum Industry. *Brooklyn Daily Eagle,* August 10, p. 11.

1920a   American Chicle's Plant Ready Soon. *Brooklyn Daily Eagle,* August 21, p. 6.

1920b   5,000,000 Packages per Day Output of New Chicle Plant. *Brooklyn Daily Eagle,* October 9, p. 9.

1923a   Wm. Wrigley Jr. Has Toxic Poisoning. *New York Times,* January 11, p. 21.

1923b   Called Klansman; Sues. *New York Times,* February 3, p. 14.

1923c   Calls Wrigley Klansman. *New York Times,* February 8, p. 16.

1924   Assail of Officers of Chicle Company: Stockholders Organize a Protective Committee and Plan to Change Management. *New York Times,* February 19, p. 26.

1926   Pirates and Rebels Active in Caribbean: Negro Band Raids Mexican Coast—Plot against Nicaragua Off Quintana Roo. *New York Times,* July 26, p. 17.

1928a   American Chicle Co. *New York Times,* November 28, p. 19.

1928b   Adams Gum. *Washington Post,* August 4, p. 6.

1929   Maya Indians Rise on Chicle: Several Dead, Many Wounded in Clashes with Employers in Quintana Roo. *New York Times,* August 22, p. 20.

1930   William J. Arkell Dies in California. *New York Times,* December 31, p. 18.

1931   Chicle Hunters of Mexico: In Quintana Roo Indians and Outlaws Live for Months on a Strange Frontier. *New York Times,* February 15, p. 84.

1932a   Wrigley Dies at 70 after Long Illness. *Washington Post,* January 27, p. 4.

1932b   Maya Ruins Found by Chicle Gatherer. *El Palacio* 19–20:258–259.

1932c   Chewing Gum Led to Mayan City Find. *New York Times*, August 16, p. 24.

1932d   Morley Describes Newly Discovered Maya Metropolis. *Washington Post*, June 9, p. 20.

1935   Chicle Trees Take Years to Recover from Knife Wounds. *Washington Post*, April 14, p. A13.

1937a   Robert H. A. Fleer. *New York Times*, January 8, p. 19.

1937b   Trotsky, Stalin, and Cardenas. *Time*, January 25. http://www.time.com/time/magazine/article/0,9171,770539,00.html (accessed October 18, 2007).

1939a   Gum Droppers. *Washington Post*, December 7, p. 12.

1939b   Mayor's Gum Drive Off to Fast Start. *New York Times*, December 11, p. 12.

1942a   Annual Meetings of Corporations: American Chicle Expects 1942 Sales to Be Only 10 to 15 Per Cent Under '41 Peak. *New York Times*, March 4, p. 31.

1942b   Blodgett Sees Reduced Sales: American Chicle Head Reports War Effects. *Brooklyn Daily Eagle*, March 4, p. 10.

1944a   Wrigley Quits as Company Head; James C. Cox Named President. *New York Times*, March 29, p. 26.

1944b   Military to Get All Wrigley Gum. *Washington Post*, April 25, p. 14.

1945   Wrigley Seeks New Sources for Gum Base. *Washington Post*, February 25, p. M8.

1946   Bartlett Arkell, Food Packer, Dies. *New York Times*, October 14, p. 22.

1947a   Mexican States Worried: May Push Output of Synthetic Gum. *New York Times*, June 20, pp. 29, 34.

1947b   Chicle Hunt Leads to Mayan Temples: Archaeologist Finds 11 Ruins, Highlighted by "Revealing" Murals, Record Stones. *New York Times*, May 22, p. 56.

1952   Guatemala Loses Trade: Her Chicle Priced Too High for the Wrigley Company. *New York Times*, July 27, p. 7.

1953   Juan del Monte: Leyenda Chiclera. *Yikal Maya Than: Revista del Literatura Maya* 14 (168) (August 31): 143–144.

1956   Horatio Adams, Gum Developer. *New York Times*, January 28, p. 17.

1960   Wrigley Patents a Novel Denture. *New York Times*, March 23, p. 56.

1973   Conferences. *Current Anthropology* 14 (4): 506–513.

1983   For Fleer Bubble Gum, Fights and Fast Moves. *New York Times*, April 4, p. D2.

1984   Nicotine Gum Approved by U.S. *New York Times*, January 18, p. A18.

2002   Singapore's Chewing Gum Ban Comes Unstuck. *BBC News* online, November 20. http://news.bbc.co.uk/2/hi/asia-pacific/2494499.stm (accessed November 1, 2007).

2007   Non-Stick Gum Something to Chew On. *Washington Post*, September 14. http://www.washingtonpost.com/wp-dyn/content/article/2007/09/14/AR2007091401741.html (accessed November 1, 2007).

Atran, Scott
1993   Itza Maya Tropical Agro-Forestry. *Current Anthropology* 34 (5): 633–700.

Atwood, Roger
2003   Guardians of the Dead. *Archaeology* 56 (1): 43–49.

Aveling, E. M., and C. Heron
1999   Chewing Tar in the Early Holocene: An Archaeological and Ethnographic Evaluation. *Antiquity* 73 (281): 579–583.

Avilan, R. L., E. G. Laborem, M. Figueroa, and L. Rangel
1980   Absorcion de Nutrimentos por una Cosecha de Nispero (*Achras sapota* L.). *Agronomia Tropical* 30 (1–6): 7–16.

Bafna, A. M., N. M. Parikh, G. B. Shah, and P. M. Bhatt
1983   Effect of Long Term Fertilization on Yield of Sapota (*Achras sapota* L) and N Fractions in Soil. *South Indian Horticulture* 31 (213): 66–69.

Balerdi C. F., J. H. Crane, and I. Maguire
2005   Fact Sheet HS-1: Sapodilla Growing in the Florida Home Landscape. Florida Cooperative Extension Service, Institute of Food and Agricultural Sciences. http://edis.ifas.ufl.edu/MG057 (accessed November 7, 2007).

Balser, Carlos
1962   Notes on Resin in Aboriginal Central America. Proceedings of the International Congress of Americanists, 34th session, Vienna.

Barbour, Thomas
1945   *A Naturalist in Cuba*. Boston: Little, Brown and Co.

Barrera de Jorgenson, Amanda
1993   Chicle Extraction and Forest Conservation in Quintana Roo, Mexico. Master's thesis, University of Florida.

Bartlett, H. H.
1935   A Method of Procedure for Field Work in Tropical American Phytogeography Based upon Botanical Reconnaissance in Parts of British Honduras and the Petén Forest in Guatemala. In *Botany of the Maya Area, Miscellaneous Papers*, Publication 461:1–26. Washington DC: Carnegie Institution.

Benton, Megan
1997   "Too Many Books": Book Ownership and Cultural Identity in the 1920s. *American Quarterly* 49 (2): 268–297.

Berdan, Frances F., and Patricia Rieff Anawalt
1992   *The Codex Mendoza*. Berkeley and Los Angeles: University of California Press.

Beteta, Ramón
1937   *Tierra del Chicle*. Mexico.

Broughton, W. J., and H. C. Wong

1979   Storage Conditions and Ripening of Chiku Fruits *Achras sapota* L. *Scientia Horticulturae* 10:377–385.

Butani, D. K.

1975   Insect Pests of Fruit Crops and Their Control: Sapota. *Pesticides* 9 (11): 37–39.

Caldwell, James R.

1980   Archaeobotanical Aspects of the 1980 Field Season. In *The Colha Project, Second Season 1980: Interim Report*, edited by Thomas R. Hester, Jack D. Eaton, and Harry J. Schafer, 257–268. Center for Archaeological Research, University of Texas, San Antonio, and Centro Studi e Ricerche Ligabue, Venice.

Campbell, C. W., S. E. Malo, and J. Popenoe

1987   Tikal: An Early-Maturing Sapodilla Cultivar. *Proceedings of the Florida State Horticultural Society* 100:281–283.

Chadha, K. L.

1992   Strategy for Optimization of Productivity and Utilization of Sapota (*Manilkara achras* (Mill.) Forberg.) *Indian Journal of Horticulture* 49 (1): 1–17.

Chandler, W. H.

1958   *Evergreen Orchards*. Philadelphia: Lea and Febiger.

Chardon, Roland

1963   Hacienda and Ejido in Yucatán: The Example of Santa Ana Cuca. *Annals of the Association of American Geographers* 53 (2): 174–193.

Chin, H. F., and E. H. Roberts

1980   *Recalcitrant Crop Seeds*. Kuala Lumpur, Malaysia: Tropical.

Chundawat, B. S., and H. P. Bhuva

1982   Performance of Some Cultivars of Sapota (*Achras sapota* L) in Gujarat. *Haryana Journal of Horticultural Sciences* 11 (3/4): 154–158.

Clarke, S. T.

1934   Investigation of Chiclero Ulcer. *Carnegie Institution of Washington, Year Book* 33:108–109.

Coe, Michael

1974   A Carved Wooden Box from the Classic Maya Civilization. In *Primera Mesa Redonda de Palenque*, pt. II, edited by Merle Greene Robison, 51–59. Pebble Beach, CA: Robert Louis Stevenson School of Pre-Columbian Art Research.

1999   *Breaking the Maya Code*. London: Thames and Hudson.

2005   *The Maya*. 7th ed. London: Thames and Hudson.

Coe, Sophie D., and Michael D. Coe
1996   *The True History of Chocolate*. London: Thames and Hudson.

Coe, William R., Edwin M. Shook, and Linton Satterthwaite
1961   Carved Wooden Lintels of Tikal. *Tikal Report* 6:15–112. Philadelphia: University of Pennsylvania, University Museum.

Coggins, Clemency Chase, and John M. Ladd
1992   Copal and Rubber Offerings. In *Artifacts from the Cenote of Sacrifice, Chichén Itzá, Yucatán*, edited by Clemency Chase Coggins, 345–357. Memoirs of the Peabody Museum of Archaeology and Ethnology, vol. 10, no. 3.

Cohn, Victor
1980   Nicotine Chewing Gum Endorsed to Help Smokers Kick the Habit. *Washington Post*, May 14, p. D8.

Collins, James H.
1927   What I Learned of Success from Successful Men. *McClure's* 59 (2): 34.
1929   Almost the Naked Truth. *Washington Post*, March 12, p. 13.

Cook, O. F.
1913   Nomenclature of the Sapota and the Sapodilla. *Contributions of the U.S National Herbarium* 16:277–285.

Crabtree, Don E.
1968   Mesoamerican Polyhedral Cores and Prismatic Blades. *American Antiquity* 33 (4): 446–478.

Cronquist, A.
1945   Studies in the Sapotaceae-IV: The North American Species of Manilkara. *Bulletin of the Torrey Botanical Club* 72 (6): 550–562.

Cruz-Rodríguez, J. A., and L. López-Mata
2004   Demography of the Seedling Bank of *Manilkara zapota* (L.) Royen, in a Subtropical Rain Forest of Mexico. *Plant Ecology* 172:227–235.

Dahl, Roald
2004[1964]   *Charlie and the Chocolate Factory*. New York City: Random House.

Dávila, Mario, and James E. Brady
2004   La Produción del Hule el Juego del Pelota. *Estudios Jalisciences* 56:40–49.

Decauville, M. Paul
1993   On Portable Railways. *Narrow Gauge and Industrial Railway Modeling Review* 2 (13): 148–160.

De la Garza, Mercedes, Ana Luisa Izquierdo, María del Carmen León, and Tolita Figueroa
1983   *Relaciones Histórico-Geográficas de la Gobernación de Yucatán (Mérida, Valladolid y Tabasco).* Mexico City: Universidad Nacional Autónoma de México.

De Los Angeles La Torre-Cuadros, M., and G. A. Islebe
2003   Traditional Ecological Knowledge and Use of Vegetation in Southeastern Mexico: A Case Study from Solferino, Quintana Roo. *Biodiversity and Conservation* 12:2455–2476.

De Morais, P.L.D., L.C.D. Lima, R. E. Alves, H.A.C. Filgueiras, and A.D.S. Almeida
2006   Physical, Physiological, and Chemical Changes during Storage of Two Sapodilla Cultivars. *Pesquisa Agropecuaria Brasileira* 41 (4): 549–554.

DeWalt, Sara J., and Jérôme Chave
2004   Structure and Biomass of Four Lowland Neotropical Forests. *Biotropica* 36:7–19.

Dibble, Charles E., and Arthur J. O. Anderson, translators
1961   Book 10: The People (no. 14, part XI). In *Florentine Codex: General History of the Things of New Spain.* Santa Fe: Monographs of the School of American Research and the Museum of New Mexico.
1963   Book 11: Earthly Things (no. 14, part XII). In *Florentine Codex: General History of the Things of New Spain.* Santa Fe: Monographs of the School of American Research and the Museum of New Mexico.

Dickson, James H., Klaus Oeggl, and Linda L. Handley
2005   The Iceman Reconsidered. *Scientific American*, special edition, 15 (1): 4–13.

Dimeglio, Steve
2001   Pieces of Cardboard, Pieces of History. *USA Today*, Baseball Weekly.com, May 1. http://www.usatoday.com/sports/bbw/2001-05-02/2001-05-02-specialtopps.htm.

Dougherty, Philip H.
1975   Gum for Your Third Set of Teeth. *New York Times*, September 19, p. 57.

Dugelby, Barbara L.
1995   Chicle Latex Extraction in the Maya Biosphere Reserve: Behavioral, Institutional, and Ecological Factors Affecting Sustainability. PhD diss., Duke University.

Edgar, W. M.
1998   Sugar Substitutes, Chewing Gum and Dental Caries—A Review. *Brazilian Dental Journal* 184 (1): 26.

Edmonds, Margot, and Ella E. Clark
1989   *Voices of the Winds: Native American Legends.* New York City: Facts on File.

Edwards, Clinton R.

1986   The Human Impact on the Forest in Quintana Roo, Mexico. *Journal of Forest History* 30 (3): 120–127.

Egler, F. E.

1947   The Role of Botanical Research in the Chicle Industry. *Economic Botany* 1:188–209.

Einbond, L. S., K. A. Reynertson, X. D. Luo, M. J. Basile, and E. J. Kennelly

2004   Anthocyanin Antioxidants from Edible Fruits. *Food Chemistry* 84:23–28.

Elden, Alfred

1926   Spruce Gum Is Still in Favor. *New York Times*, May 9, p. XX5.

Escalona Ramos, Alberto

1940   Las Vías de Comunicación en Quintana Roo. *Revista Mexicana de Geografía* 1:207–229.

Espejel, I.

1987   A Phytogeographical Analysis of Coastal Vegetation in the Yucatán Peninsula. *Journal of Biogeography* 14 (6): 499–519.

Everton, Macduff

1991   *The Modern Maya: A Culture in Transition*. Albuquerque: University of New Mexico Press.

Fægri, V., and L. van der Pijl

1971   *Principles of Pollination Ecology*. 2nd ed. Oxford: Pergamon.

Farnsworth, Elizabeth

2000   The Ecology and Physiology of Viviparous and Recalcitrant Seeds. *Annual Review of Ecology and Systematics* 31:107–138.

Farooqi, A. A., and M. M. Rao

1976   Studies on Metaxenia in Sapota. *Mysore Journal of Agricultural Science* 10 (3): 413–423.

Feld, Rose C.

1925   Chewing-Gum King's Rise a Modern Business Romance. *New York Times*, March 1, p. XX5.

Fleming, T. H.

1988   *The Short-Tailed Fruit Bat: A Study in Plant-Animal Interactions*. Chicago: University of Chicago Press.

Fleming-Michael, Karen
2006   Caffeine Gum Now in Army Supply Channels. *AR News*, January 6. http://www4
.army.mil/ocpa/read.php?story_id_key=8471 (accessed November 1, 2007).

Flynn, S., R. M. Turner, and W. H. Stuppy
2006   Seed Information Database (release 7.0, Oct. 2006). http://www.kew.org/data/sid
(accessed November 1, 2007).

Folan, William J., Laraine A. Fletcher, and Ellen R. Kintz
1979   Fruit, Fiber, Bark, and Resin: Social Organization of a Maya Urban Center. *Science*
204 (4394): 697–701.

Forbes 400 Richest Americans
2006   http://www.forbes.com/lists/2007/54/richlist07_The-400-Richest-Americans_
NameProper_16.html (accessed November 1, 2007).

Forero, Oscar A., and Michael R. Redclift
2006   The Role of the Mexican State in the Development of *Chicle* Extraction in Yucatán,
and the Continuing Importance of *Coyotaje*. *Journal of Latin American Studies*
38:61–93.

Fosberg, F. R.
1964   The Correct Name of the Chicle Tree. *Taxon* 13:254–255.

Fox, David A.
1961   Henequen in Yucatán: A Mexican Fibre Crop. *Transactions and Papers (Institute
of British Geographers)* 29:215–229.

Gandhi, S. R.
1956   *The Chiku in India*. New Delhi: Indian Council of Agricultural Research.

Gann, Thomas W. F.
1918   The Maya Indians of Southern Yucatán and Northern British Honduras, Smith-
sonian Institution. *Bureau of Indian Ethnology Bulletin*, No. 64. Washington DC:
U.S. Government Printing Office.

Gentry, A. H.
1995   Diversity and Floristic Composition of Neotropical Dry Forests. In *Seasonally Dry
Tropical Forests*, edited by S. H. Bullock, H. A. Mooney, and E. Medina, 146–190.
Cambridge: Cambridge University Press.

Gilly, C. L.
1943   Studies in the Sapotaceae, II. The Sapodilla-Nispero Complex. *Tropical Woods*
73:1–22.

González, L. G., and P. A. Feliciano Jr.
1953   The Blooming and Fruiting Habits of the Ponderosa Chico. *Philippine Agriculture* 37 (7): 384–398.

Goodnough, Amy
1998   W. E. Diemer, Bubble Gum Inventor, Dies at 93. *New York Times*, January 12, p. B7.

Greenhall, A. M.
1957   Food Preferences of Trinidad Fruit Bats. *Journal of Mammalogy* 38 (3): 409–410.

Gustaitis, Joseph
1998   The Sticky History of Chewing Gum. *American History* 33:30–34, 69–71.

Hammond, Norman K., Anne Pyburn, John Rose, J. C. Staneko, and Deborah Muyskens
1986   Excavation and Survey at Nohmul, Belize, 1986. *Journal of Field Archaeology* 15 (1): 1–15.

Hammonds, Keith
1982   In Baseball Cards, Topps Still Leads the League. *New York Times*, April 25, p. 155.

Hanighen, Frank C.
1934   *Santa Anna: The Napoleon of the West*. New York City: Coward-McCann.

Hansen, Richard D.
1997   Plundering the Petén. *Archaeology* 50 (5): 48–49.

Hart, N. K., J. A. Lamberton, and A.C.K. Triffett
1973   Triterpenoids of *Achras sapota* (Sapotaceae). *Australian Journal of Chemistry* 26 (8): 1827–1829.

Hastorf, Christine A.
1991   Gender, Space, and Food in Prehistory. In *Engendering Archaeology*, edited by Joan M. Gero and Meg W. Conkey, 132–159. Cambridge: Blackwell.

Heaton, Hoyt J.
1997   A Study of Variation in Chicozapote (*Manilkara zapota*). Master's thesis, University of California, Riverside.

Heaton, Hoyt J., R. Whitkus, and Arturo Gómez-Pompa
1999   Extreme Ecological and Phenotypic Differences in the Tropical Tree Chicozapote (*Manilkara zapota* (L.) van Royen) Are Not Matched by Genetic Divergence: A RAPD Analysis. *Molecular Ecology* 8:627–632.

Heithaus, Raymond, E., T. H. Fleming, and P. A. Opler
1975   Foraging Patterns and Resource Utilization in Seven Species of Bats in a Seasonal Tropical Forest. *Ecology* 56 (4): 841–854.

Hendrickson, Robert
1976   *The Great American Chewing Gum Book*. Rodnor, PA: Chilton Book Company.

Hernández, Francisco
1959   *Historia Natural de Nueva España*. Vol. 1. Mexico City: Universidad Nacional de México.

Hernández, Silvia
2008   Mayas "Pegan" su Chicle en Europa. El Universal.com. http://www.eluniversal.com.mx/estados/vi_68206.html (accessed April 21, 2008).

Heyder, H. M.
1930   Sapodilla Tapping in British Honduras. *Empire Forestry Journal* 9 (1): 107–113.

Higbee, Edward
1948   Agriculture in the Maya Homeland. *Geographical Review* 38 (3): 457–464.

Hoar, H. M.
1924   Chicle and Chewing Gum: A Review of Chicle Production and Sources of Supply, and the Chewing Gum Industry and Trade. *Trade Information Bulletin* 197:1–10.

Hodder, Ian
1985   Postprocessual Archaeology. In *Advances in Archaeological Method and Theory*, vol. 8, edited by Michael B. Schiffer, 1–26. New York City: Academic Press.

Hodge, Robert H.
1955   The Chewing Gum Tree. *Natural History* 64:74–80.

Hollingworth, H. L.
1939   The Psycho-Dynamics of Chewing. *New York: Archives of Psychology*, no. 239 (July): 5–89.

Hubbard, Elbert
1998   *Preachments: Elbert Hubbard's Selected Writings, Part 4*. Whitefish, MT: Kessinger Publishing.

Hussain, A., and M. A. Bukhari
1977   Performance of Different Grafting Methods in Chiku *Achras sapota*. *Pakistan Journal of Botany* 9 (1): 47–57.

Iruegas, Rubén, Benigno Gómez, Leopoldo Cruz-López, Edi A. Malo, and Julio C. Rojas
2002   A New Record of a Moth Attacking Sapodilla, with Descriptions of Female Genitalia and the Last Instar Larva. *Florida Entomologist* 85:394–397.

Jain, R. K., and S. K. Jain
1998　Sensory Evaluation of an Intermediate Moisture Product from "Sapota" (*Achras zapota* L.). *Journal of Food Engineering* 37:323–330.

Karling, John S.
1934　Dendrograph Studies on *Achras zapota* in Relation to the Optimum Conditions for Tapping. *American Journal of Botany* 21 (4): 161–193.
1935　*Couama guatemalensis* as a Possible Future Source of Chicle. *American Journal of Botany* 22 (6): 580–593.
1942a　Collecting Chicle in the American Tropics, Part I. *Torreya* 42:38–49.
1942b　Collecting Chicle in the American Tropics, Part 2. *Torreya* 42:69–82.
1942c　The Response of *Achras zapota* in Latex Yield to Wounding by the Ibidem Method of Tapping. *Bulletin of the Torrey Botanical Club* 69 (8): 553–560.

Kashanipour, R. A., and R. J. McGee
2004　Northern Lacandon Maya Medicinal Plant Use in the Communities of Lacanja Chan Sayab and Naha', Chiapas, Mexico. *Journal of Ecological Anthropology* 8:47–66.

Khare, V., P. Mehta, M. Kachhwaha, and A. Mehta
1994　Role of Phenolic Substances in Pathogenesis of Soft Rot Diseases. *Journal of Basic Microbiology* 34 (5): 323–328.

Kim, Warren Y.
1971　*Koreans in America.* Seoul: Po Chin Chai Printing.

King, Seth
1971　Wrigley: A 7-Cent Bonanza. *New York Times*, May 9, p. F1.

Klimstra, W. D., and A. L. Dooley
1990　Foods of the Key Deer. *Florida Scientist* 53 (4): 264–273.

Konrad, Herman W.
1987　Capitalismo y Trabajo en los Bosques de las Tierras Bajas Tropicales Mexicanas: El Caso de la Industria del Chicle. *História Mexicana* 36 (3): 465–505.
1991　Capitalism on the Tropical-Forest Frontier: Quintana Roo, 1880s to 1930. In *Land, Labor, and Capital in Modern Yucatán: Essays in Regional History and Political Economy*, edited by Jeffery T. Brannon and Gilbert M. Joseph, 143–171. Tuscaloosa: University of Alabama Press.
1995　Maya Chicleros and the International Chewing Gum Market. In *The Fragmented Present: Mesoamerican Societies Facing Modernization*, edited by Ruth Gubler and Ueli Hostettler, 97–114. Moeckmuehl, Germany: A. Surwein.

Kute, L. S., and M. B. Shete

1995   Sapota (Sapodilla). In *Handbook of Fruit Science and Technology*, edited by D. K. Salunkhe and S. S. Kadam, 475–484. New York City: Marcel Dekker.

Laborem E., Gastón, Maximiano Figueroa, Omar Verde, Luis Rangel, and Luis Bandres

1981   Efecto de La Fertilizacion con N, P, y K Sobre Los Rendimientos de Nispero (*Manilkara achras*) en Suelos del Orden Entisol. *Agronomía Tropical* 31 (1–6): 31–36.

Lakshminarayana, S.

1980   Sapodilla and Prickly Pear. In *Tropical and Subtropical Fruit: Composition, Properties, and Uses*, edited by Steven Nagy, Philip E. Shaw, and Wilfred F. Wardowski, 415–441. Westport, CT: AVI Publishing.

Lakshminarayana, S., and H. Subramanyam

1966   Physical, Chemical, and Physiological Changes in Sapota Fruit [*Achras sapota* Linn. (Sapotaceae)] during Development and Ripening. *Journal of Food Science and Technology* 3:151–154.

Lambert, J.D.H., and J. T. Arnason

1982   *Ramón* and Maya Ruins: An Ecological, Not an Economic, Relation. *Science* 216 (16): 298–299.

Landon, Charles

1935   The Chewing Gum Industry. *Economic Geography* 11 (2): 183–190.

Langenheim, Jean H.

2003   *Plant Resins: Chemistry, Evolution, Ecology, and Ethnobotany*. Portland, OR: Timber Press.

Lanigan-Schmidt, Therese

2003   *Ghosts of New York City*. Atglen, PA: Schiffer.

Lans, C., T. Harper, K. Georges, and E. Bridgewater

2000   Medicinal Plants Used on Dogs in Trinidad and Tobago. *Preventative Veterinary Medicine* 45 (3–4): 201–220.

Lentz, David L.

1990   *Acrocomia mexicana*: Palm of the Ancient Mesoamericans. *Journal of Ethnobiology* 10:183–194.

Lizardi Ramos, César

1937a   El Corte de Caoba y la Producción de Chicle en Quintana Roo. *Excelsior*, October 24, pp. 2, 3, 4.

1937b   Cómo son y Cómo Viven los Chicleros de Quintana Roo. *Excelsior*, November 14, pp. 1, 3.

Lothrop, Samuel Kirkland
1937   *Coclé: Archaeological Study of Central Panama.* Memoirs of the Peabody Museum of Archaeology and Ethnology 7. Cambridge, MA: Peabody Museum.

Lundell, Cyrus L.
1933a   Chicle Exploitation in the Sapodilla Forest of the Yucatán Peninsula. *Field and Laboratory* 2 (1): 15–21.
1933b   Archaeological Discoveries in the Maya Area. *Proceedings of the American Philosophical Society* 72 (3): 147–179.
1937   *The Vegetation of Petén.* Carnegie Institution of Washington Publication 478. Washington DC.
1968   Undescribed Species and Notes on Other Plants from Middle America. *Phytologia* 16 (5): 442–446.
1977   Studies of American Plants XIV. *Wrightia* 5 (9): 331–351.
1978   Studies of American Plants XVI. *Wrightia* 6 (1): 12–17.

Ma, J., X. D. Luo, P. Protiva, H. Yang, C. Ma, M. J. Basile, I. B. Weinstein, and E. J. Kennelly
2003   Bioactive Novel Polyphenols from the Fruit of *Manilkara zapota* (Sapodilla). *Journal of Natural Products* 66:983–986.

Mabberley, D. J.
1997   *The Plant Book: A Portable Dictionary of the Vascular Plants.* 2nd ed. Cambridge: Cambridge University Press.

Macías Zapata, Gabriel A.
1992   Soldados, Indios, y Libre Comercio en Quintana Roo, 1893–1903. *Relaciones: Estudios de Historia y Sociedad* 12 (49): 129–152.

Madhava-Rao, T. N., R. B. Gowder, and R. Venkatraman
1975   New Sapotas from Coimbatore. *Indian Horticulture* 20 (1): 7–8.

Martin, David
2008   Mars Offers $23 Billion Cash for Wrigley. *New York Times,* April 29. http://www.nytimes.com/2008/04/29/business/29wrigley.html?scp=2&sq=wrigley+gum&st=nyt (accessed May 13, 2008).

Martín del Campo, David
1999   *Chicle: Los Artistas del Machete.* Mexico City: Sedesol.

Mathews, Jennifer P., and Lilia Lizama-Rogers
2005   Jungle Rails: A Narrow Gauge Railway in Quintana Roo, Mexico. In *Quintana Roo Archaeology,* edited by Justine M. Shaw and Jennifer P. Mathews, 112–126. Tucson: University of Arizona Press.

McCafferty, Sharisse D., and Geoffrey G. McCafferty
1991   Spinning and Weaving as Female Gender Identity in Post-Classic Mexico. In *Textile Traditions of Mesoamerica and the Andes: An Anthology*, edited by Margot Blum Schevill, Janet Catherine Berlo, and Edward B. Dwyer, 19–49. New York City: Garland.

McCormacls, Patricia
1975   Kicking the Habit, By Gum. *Washington Post*, June 8, p. 156.

McKillop, Heather
1994   Ancient Maya Tree Cropping: A Viable Subsistence Adaptation for the Island Maya. *Ancient Mesoamerica* 5:129–140.

McNab, Roan Balas
1998   Comparative Impacts of Chicle and Xate Harvests on Wildlife of the Maya Biosphere Reserve, Guatemala. Master's thesis, University of Florida.

Medina-Gaud, S., F. Gallardo Covas, E. Abreu, and R. Ingles
1987   The Insects of Nispero (*Manilkara zapota* (L.) P. van Royen) in Puerto Rico. *Journal of Agriculture of the University of Puerto Rico* 71 (1): 129–132.

Menéndez, Gabriel Antonio
1936   *Quintana Roo: Album Monográfico*. Mexico City.

Mickelbart, M. V.
1996   Sapodilla: A Potential Crop for Subtropical Climates. In *Progress in New Crops*, edited by Jules Janick, 439–446. Alexandria, VA: ASHS Press.

Mickelbart, M. V., and T. E. Marler
1996   Photosynthesis, Water Relations, and Mineral Content of Sapodilla Foliage as Influenced by Root Zone Salinity. *HortScience* 31:230–233.

Miksicek, Charles H., Kathryn J. Elsseser, Ingrid A. Wuebber, Karen Olsen Brunhns, and Norman Hammond
1981   Rethinking Ramón: A Comment on Reina and Hill's Lowland Maya Subsistence. *American Antiquity* 46 (4): 916–919.

Miller, Mary Ellen
1986   *The Murals of Bonampak*. Princeton, NJ: Princeton University Press.

Mitgang, Herbert
1959   Cardboard League. *New York Times*, September 20, pp. SM75–SM76.

Mohawk Valley Library System
1999   http://www.mvls.info/lhg/canajo/6.html (accessed November 1, 2007).

Molina Montes, Augusto F.

1978   Palenque: The Archaeological City Today. In *Tercera Mesa Redonda de Palenque, 1978*, edited by Merle Greene Robertson and Donnan C. Jeffers, 1–8. Monterrey, Mexico: Pre-Columbian Art Research Center.

Möller, Harry

1986   Un Ferrocarril que Nadie Quiere Recordar. *México Desconocido*, no. 111:36–40.

Montiel, Salvador, Alejandro Estrada, and Perla León

2006   Bat Assemblages in a Naturally Fragmented Ecosystem in the Yucatán Peninsula, Mexico: Species Richness, Diversity, and Spatio-Temporal Dynamics. *Journal of Tropical Ecology* 22:267–276.

Moore, Anne

2005   Wrigley. *Crain's Chicago Business* 28 (42): 40.

Moore, H. E., and W. T. Stearn

1967   The Identity of *Achras zapota* L., and the Names for the Sapodilla and the Sapote. *Taxon* 16:382–395.

Morehart, Christopher T., David L. Lentz, and Keith M. Prufer

2005   Wood of the Gods: The Ritual Use of Pine (*Pinus* spp.) by the Ancient Lowland Maya. *Latin American Antiquity* 16 (3): 255–274.

Morley, Sylvanus Griswald

1943   Symposium on Recent Advances in American Archaeology: Archaeological Investigations of the Carnegie Institution of Washington in the Maya Area of Middle America, during the Past Twenty-Eight Years. *Proceedings of the American Philosophical Society* 86 (2): 205–219.

Morrone, Francis

2001   *The Architectural Guidebook to Brooklyn*. Layton, UT: Gibbs Smith Publisher.

Morrow, James B.

1908   George Herber Worthington Tells of Evolution of Chewing Gum Trust. *Washington Post*, November 29, p. E1.

Morton, Julia F.

1987   *Fruits of Warm Climates*. Winterville, NC: Creative Resources Systems.

Mulla, A. L., and G. Y. Desle

1990   Pollination Studies in Sapota Cultivars. *Journal of Maharashtra Agricultural University* 15 (2): 266–268.

Mutchnick, P. A., and B. C. McCarthy

1997   An Ethnobotanical Analysis of the Tree Species Common to the Subtropical Moist Forests of the Petén, Guatemala. *Economic Botany* 51:158–183.

Nadal, Laura Filloy

1999   Rubber and Rubber Balls in Mesoamerica. In *The Sport of Life and Death: The Mesoamerican Ballgame*, edited by E. Michael Whittington, 20–31. London: Thames and Hudson.

Neale, Andrew

1992   Paul Decauville and the Portable Railway. *Narrow Gauge and Industrial Railway Modelling Review* 2 (13): 146–147.

Neumeister, Larry

2006   Bazooka Recipe Open to Foreign Gum Maker. Associated Press, September 4. http://www.cbsnews.com/stories/2006/09/04/ap/business/mainD8JU8SG02.shtml (accessed November 1, 2007).

Nichols, Lewis

1930   American Chewing Gum Has Taken Hold Abroad: The War Carried It to Europe, and Foreigners Now Make It, and Their Use of It Is Growing. *New York Times*, June 15, p. X12.

Noyes, Jesse

2006   New Bazooka Joe Something to Chew On. *Boston Herald*, March 29, p. 3.

O'Farrill, G., S. Calme, and A. González

2006   *Manilkara zapota*: A New Record of a Species Dispersed by Tapirs. *Tapir Conservation* 15 (1): 32–35.

Ogden, M.A.H., and C. W. Campbell

1980   Wild Dilly as a Potential Rootstock for Sapodilla. *Proceedings of the Tropical Region, American Society for Horticultural Science* 24:89–92.

Orellana, S. L.

1987   *Indian Medicine in Highland Guatemala*. Albuquerque: University of New Mexico Press.

Ortega Canto, Judith, Jolly Hoil Santos, and Angél Ledenchy Grajales

1996   *Leishmaniasis en Milperos de Campeche (una Aproimación Médico-Antopológica)*. Folleto de Investigación 5. Universidad Autónoma de Yucatán, Mexico.

Patch, Robert W.

1993   *Maya and Spaniard in Yucatán, 1648–1812*. Palo Alto, CA: Stanford University Press.

Patil, V. K., and P. R. Narwadkar
1974   Studies on Flowering, Pollination, Fruit Set, and Fruit Drop in Chiku. *Punjab Horticultural Journal* 14 (1–2): 39–42.

Patterson, Wayne
2000   *The Ilse: First-Generation Korean Immigrants in Hawaii, 1903–1973*. Honolulu: University of Hawaii Press.

Peissel, Michel
1963   *The Lost World of Quintana Roo*. New York City: E. P. Dutton.

Pennington, T. D.
1990   Sapotaceae. *Flora Neotropica*. Monograph 52. New York City: New York Botanical Garden.
1991   *The Genera of Sapotaceae*. New York City: New York Botanical Garden.

Pérez-Arbelaez, E.
1956   *Plantas Utiles de Colombia*. Bogotá: Libreria Colombiana.

Peters, C. M., B. G. Bagle, and R. Balasubramanian
1984   A New Record of Scolytid Beetles as a Pest of Sapota. *Current Research, University of Agricultural Science, Bangalore* 13:7.

Phillips, McCandlish
1964   Cards with Gum: A Money Bubble. *New York Times*, February 24, pp. 27, 49.

Piatos, P., and R. J. Knight
1975   Self-Incompatibility in the Sapodilla. *Proceedings of the Florida State Horticultural Society* 88:464–465.

Plan Piloto Chiclero
1998   *El Chicle*. Video recording. Chetumal, Mexico: Cinergia Multimedia S. A. de C. V.

Pliny
1968   *Natural History*. Translated by H. Rackham. Vol. 4. Cambridge, MA: Harvard University Press.

Plumier, C.
1703   *Nova Plantarum Americanarum Genera*. Paris.

Post, Elizabeth L.
1969   *Emily Post's Etiquette*. 12th rev. ed. New York: Funk and Wagnalls.

Post, Emily
1956   *Etiquette: The Blue Book of Social Usage*. New York: Funk and Wagnalls.

Post, Peggy

2004   *Emily Post's Etiquette*. 17th ed. New York: Harper Resource.

Puleston, Dennis E.

1982   Role of Ramón in Maya Subsistence. In *Maya Subsistence: Studies in Memory of Dennis E. Puleston*, edited by Kent V. Flannery, 353–364. New York City: Academic Press.

Purohit, S. D., and A. Singhvi

1998   Micropropagation of *Achras sapota* through Enhanced Axillary Branching. *Scientia Horticulturae* 76:219–229.

Redclift, Michael

2003   Chewing Gum and the Shadowlands of Consumption. *Revista Mexicana del Caribe* 15:159–167.

2004   *Chewing Gum: The Fortunes of Taste*. New York City: Routledge.

Reddi, E.U.B.

1989   Thrips Pollination in Sapodilla (*Manilkara zapota*). *Proceedings of the Indian National Science Academy* B55 (5–6): 407–410.

Reed, Nelson

1964   *The Caste War of Yucatán*. Palo Alto, CA: Stanford University Press.

Reese-Taylor, Kathryn

n.d.   Naachtun: A Lost City of the Maya. http://www.bbc.co.uk/history/archaeology/excavations_techniques/maya_naachtun_08.shtml (accessed November 1, 2007).

Relekar, P. P., A. G. Desai, J. C. Rajput, and M. J. Slavi

1991   Fruit Production in Sapota (cv. Kalipatti). *Current Research, University of Agricultural Science, Bangalore* 20 (6): 104–106.

Rogers, Will

1923   Remodeled Chewing Gum. *Washington Post*, December 9, p. 80.

Roys, Ralph L.

1931   *The Ethno-Botany of the Maya*. New Orleans: Tulane University.

Rubinstein, Anne

1976   Kicking the Tobacco Habit with "Nicotine Gum." *Washington Post*, September 3, p. B5.

Rubio-Espina, E.

1968   Estudio Preliminar de los Insectos Perjudiciales a los Árboles de Níspero (*Achras zapota* Linnaeus) en el Estado Zulia, Venezuela. *Revista Facul. Agronomía* 1:1–24.

Rugeley, Terry
1996   *Yucatán's Maya Peasantry and the Origins of the Caste War*. Austin: University of Texas Press.

Rugeley, Terry, editor
2001   *Maya Wars: Ethnographic Accounts from Nineteenth-Century Yucatán*. Norman: University of Oklahoma Press.

Ruppert, Karl
1947   Bonampak Expedition. *Carnegie Institution of Washington, Year Book* 46:177–179.
1955   The History of the Site of Bonampak. In *Bonampak, Chiapas, Mexico*, edited by Karl Ruppert, J. Eric S. Thompson, and Tatiana Proskouriakoff, 8–15. Carnegie Institution of Washington, Publication 602. Washington DC.

Ruppert, Karl, and John Denison Jr.
1943   *Archaeological Reconnaissance in Campeche, Quintana Roo and Petén*. Carnegie Institution of Washington, Publication 543. Washington DC.

Sahagún, Fray Bernardino
1979a   *Códice Florentino de Fray Bernardino de Sahagún*. Book 10. Mexico City: Secretaría de Gobernación.
1979b   *Códice Florentino de Fray Bernardino de Sahagún*. Book 11. Mexico City: Secretaría de Gobernación.

Sandermann, W., and H. Funke
1970   Resistance of Old Maya Temple Woods to Termites due to Saponins. *Naturwissenschaften* 57:407–414.

Scheina, Robert L.
2002   *Santa Anna: A Curse upon Mexico*. Washington DC: Brassey's.

Schele, Linda, and Peter Mathews
1998   *The Code of Kings: The Language of Seven Sacred Maya Temples and Tombs*. New York: Simon and Schuster.

Schuster, Andrea
1999   Maya Art Return. *Archaeology* 52 (1). http://www.archaeology.org/9901/news-briefs/maya.html (accessed November 1, 2007).

Schwartz, Norman B.
1974   Milperos, Chicleros, and Rituals of Passage in El Petén, Guatemala. *Cultures et Développement: Revue Internationale des Sciences du Développement* 6 (2): 369–395.

1987   Colonization of Northern Guatemala: The Petén. *Journal of Anthropological Research* 43 (2): 163–183.

1990   *Forest Society: A Social History of Petén, Guatemala.* Philadelphia: University of Pennsylvania Press.

Shattuck, George C.

1933   Life in the Forests of Quintana Roo. In *The Peninsula of Yucatán: Medical, Biological, Meteorological, and Sociological Studies,* 157–179. Washington DC: Carnegie Institution of Washington.

Shui, G., S. P. Wong, and L. P. Leong

2004   Characterization of Antioxidants and Change of Antioxidant Levels during Storage of *Manilkara zapota* L. *Journal of Agricultural and Food Chemistry* 2:7834–7841.

Simms, Greg, Jr.

2003   Hey Joe, Where Are You Going with That Gum in Your Hand? Bazooka's One-Eyed Bad Boy of Bubbles is 50 Years Old. *Dayton Daily News,* September 29, p. E1.

Simpson, B. B., and M. C. Ogorzaly

2001   *Economic Botany: Plants in Our World.* New York City: McGraw-Hill.

Singh, G., J. C. Dagar, and N. T. Singh

1997   Growing Fruit Trees in Highly Alkali Soils—A Case Study. *Land Degradation and Development* 8:257–268.

Smith, E.H.G.

1940   Chicle, Jelutong, and Allied Materials. *Bulletin of the Imperial Institute* 38:299–320.

Sohn, Emily

2007   Chew on This: It's for Your Health. *Los Angeles Times,* February 19, F1.

Sorkin, Andrew Ross

2008   Mars Reportedly Near Deal to Acquire Wrigley. *New York Times,* April 28. http://www.nytimes.com/2008/04/28/business/28wrigley.html?scp=1&sq=wrigley+gum&st=nyt (accessed May 13, 2008).

Southern Fruit Research Institute (SOFRI)

2002   *Fruits in Vietnam.* Ho Chi Minh City: Agriculture Publishing House.

Stamler, Bernard

2001   Advertising: Topps Uses Mickey Mantle, Old-Style Cards, and Bubble Gum to Help Sales and Celebrate 50 Years. *New York Times,* March 22, p. C6.

Standley, P. C.

1930   *Flora of Yucatán*. Field Museum of Natural History Botanical Series, publication 279. 3:157–492.

Stanford, Ernest Elwood

1934   *Economic Plants*. New York City: D. Appleton-Century.

Stone, Andrea

2002   Spirals, Ropes, and Feathers: The Iconography of Rubber Balls in Mesoamerican Art. *Ancient Mesoamerica* 13 (1): 21–39.

Stratton, Dorothy C., and Helen B. Schleman

1955   *Your Best Foot Forward: Social Usage for Young Moderns*. Rev. ed. New York: McGraw-Hill.

Stross, Brian

1996   Mesoamerican Copal Resins. *U Mut Maya* 6:177–186.

Sullivan, Paul

1989   *Unfinished Conversations: Mayas and Foreigners between Two Wars*. New York City: Knopf.

Tarkanian, Michael J., and Dorothy Hosler

1999   An Ancient Tradition Continued: Modern Rubber Processing in Mexico. In *The Sport of Life and Death: The Mesoamerican Ballgame*, edited by E. Michael Whittington, 116–121. London: Thames and Hudson.

Thompson, J. Eric S.

1961   Notes on a Plumbate Vessel with Shell Inlay and on Chiclero's Ulcer. In *Essays in Pre-Columbian Art and Archaeology*, edited by Samuel K. Lothrop, 171–175. Cambridge: Harvard University Press.

Topps History

2004   About Topps webpage. http://www.topps.com/AboutTopps/history.html (accessed November 1, 2007).

Torquemada, Fray Juan de

1977   *Monarquía Indiana: De los Viente y un Libros Rituales y Occidentales, de sus Poblaciones, Descubrimiento, Conquista, Conversión y otras Cosas Marvaillosas de la Mesme Tierra*. Vol. 4. Mexico City: Universidad Nacional Autónoma de México.

Torres, Vicente Francisco

2003   Sicte: La Tragedia del Chicle de los Maya. *Siempre!* November 2, pp. 72–73.

Tower, Samuel A.

1976   Stamps: Bicentennial Issues—Then and Now. *New York Times*, August 22, p. 92.

Tozzer, Alfred M.
1966   *Landa's Relación de las Cosas de Yucatán, a Translation.* Millwood, NY: Kraus Reprint.

Triplett, Kirsten Hill
1999   The Ethnobotany of Plant Resins in the Maya Cultural Region of Southern Mexico and Central America. PhD diss., University of Texas at Austin.

Tropicos Database of the Missouri Botanic Garden
2006   http://mobot.mobot.org/W3T/Search/vast.html (accessed November 2, 2007).

Tucha, Oliver, Lara Mecklinger, Kerstin Maier, Marianne Hammerl, and Klaus W. Lange
2004   Chewing Gum Differentially Affects Aspects of Attention in Healthy Subjects. *Appetite* 42 (3): 327–329.

Tweddle, John C., John B. Dickei, C. C. Baskin, and J. M. Baskin
2003   Ecological Aspects of Seed Desiccation Sensitivity. *Journal of Ecology* 91:294–304.

U.S. Bureau of the Census
1880   Ninth U.S. Census. Population Schedule. Inhabitants in Brooklyn, in the County of Kings, New York State. Department of Commerce, Bureau of the Census.

U.S. Bureau of the Census
1920   Fifteenth U.S. Census. Population Schedule. Inhabitants of Brooklyn, in the County of Kings, New York State. Department of Commerce, Bureau of the Census.

Vadillo López, Claudio
2001   *Los Chicleros en la Región de Laguna de Términos, Campeche: 1890–1947.* Cuidad del Carmen, Campeche, Mexico: Universidad Autónoma del Carmen.

Van Gelder, Lawrence
1975   Topps Called Off Base. *New York Times*, July 10, p. 33.

Van Mele, P., and T. T. Cuc Nguyen
2001   Farmers' Perceptions and Practices in Use of *Dolichoderus thoracicus* (Smith) (Hymenoptera: Formicidae) for Biological Control of Pests of Sapodilla. *Biological Control* 20:23–29.

Vélez-Colon, R., I. Beauchamp de Caloni, and S. Martinez-Garrastazu
1989   Sapodilla (*Manilkara sapota* L. V. Rogen, *Achras sapota* Linn.) Variety Trials at Southern Puerto Rico. *Journal of the Agricultural University of Puerto Rico* 73 (3): 255–264.

Villa R., Alfonso

1945   *The Maya of East Central Quintana Roo*. Washington DC: Carnegie Institution of Washington.

Virtual Herbarium at the New York Botanical Garden

2006   http://sciweb.nybg.org/science2/VirtualHerbarium.asp (accessed November 1, 2007).

Wald, Eliot

1979   Build a Better Vending Machine . . . and, Well, the Rest Is History. *Washington Post*, June 3, p. A1.

Waller, George R.

2000   Saponins. http://www.accessscience.com (DOI 10.1036/1097-8542.YB980680) (accessed November 1, 2007).

Wardlaw, Lee

1997   *Bubblemania: The Chewy History of Bubble Gum*. New York City: Aladdin.

Whigham, Dennis F., James F. Lynch, and Matthew B. Dickinson

1998   Dynamics and Ecology of Natural and Managed Forests in Quintana Roo, Mexico. In *Timber, Tourists, and Temples: Conservation and Development in the Maya Forest of Belize, Guatemala, and México*, edited by Richard B. Primack, David Barton Bray, Hugo A. Galletti, and Ismael Pinciano, 267–281. Covelo, CA: Island Press.

Wilkinson, Lucy, Andrew Scholey, and Keith Wesnes

2002   Chewing Gum Selectively Improves Aspects of Memory in Healthy Volunteers. *Appetite* 38 (3): 235–236.

Young, Emma

2002   Chewing Gum Improves Memory. New Scientist.com, March 13. http://www.newscientist.com/article/dn2039.html (accessed November 1, 2007).

Young, Robert

1990   *The Chewing Gum Book*. Minneapolis: Dillon Press.

INDEX

ABOUT THE AUTHORS

Jennifer P. Mathews has a BA from San Diego State University and an MA and PhD from the University of California, Riverside, in anthropology, with a specialization in Maya archaeology. She has conducted archaeological fieldwork in Quintana Roo, Mexico, since 1993, and is currently the codirector of the Yalahau Regional Human Ecology Project. Her recent publications include several journal articles, as well as two coedited volumes for the University of Arizona Press: *Quintana Roo Archaeology* (with Justine M. Shaw), and *Lifeways in the Northern Maya Lowlands: New Approaches to Archaeology in the Yucatán Peninsula* (with Bethany A. Morrison). Her research interests include ancient Maya architecture, site layout, road systems, historic archaeology, and current issues that indigenous peoples are facing with the rise of tourism and interest in archaeological resources. She is an associate professor at Trinity University in San Antonio, Texas, where she teaches courses in archaeology and physical anthropology.

Gillian P. Schultz has a BA from the University of Rochester and an MS and PhD from the University of California, Riverside, in botany, with a specialization in tropical ecology and plant diversity. She has conducted fieldwork on plants and animals in the Yucatán Peninsula and is currently working on a flora of the El Eden Ecological Reserve in northern Quintana Roo, Mexico. Her research interests include plant-animal interactions, plant diversity and conservation, biogeography, and human impacts on ecosystems. She is currently a member of the biology faculty at Foothill College in Los Altos Hills, California.